Ms. Celeste,

I hope you can enjoy some of these 'true life' stories, while you are relaxing this summer. Thank you for all your help with our students in TK this year! You always made it a special time when we visited you for "storytime"

Warming thoughts always,

Mr. Ward.

P. O. Box 585
Mount Shasta, California 96067

LIFE WITH
BIGFOOT

PHIL WARD

With illustrations by Lyalle E. Hegseth

ACKNOWLEDGEMENTS

The following individuals have contributed significantly to the fact that this book has become a reality. My sincerest thanks to:

Dana Conant of Quicksilver Productions, for her creation of the cover of this book and for the final format;

Lyalle L. Hegseth, for his cooperation and cartooning ability;

Phil McCracken, for his enthusiastic and helpful advice related to self-publishing details and encouragement;

Marguerite Brewster and my son, Phil, for their expertise and willingness to assist in editing;

Bobbie Richardson, for the back cover photograph;

Four wonderful sons: Jeffrey, Gregory, Phillip, and Michael, who encouraged me to record these anecdotes for posterity;

Numerous friends and guests of our Bigfoot Ranch B&B for their pre-reading and encouragement to pursue the stories herein.

INTRODUCTION

This is a compilation of true experiences based on the recent lives of a middle-aged couple who, after raising four sons, left their suburban home, "burned their bridges" behind them, and moved to a small ranch in Northern California.

The touching, and often amusing, even hilarious experiences since their arrival at their Bigfoot Ranch will provide the reader with some light-hearted entertainment and self-imposed chuckles. The book has been written because numerous friends and relatives have suggested that these stories be shared.

(Barbara and Phil Ward, retired educators, presently own Wards' Bigfoot Ranch Bed and Breakfast located two miles northwest of Mt. Shasta City, California.)

Bigfoot's Keeper

One of our sons and his family live half an hour north of our ranch. They were visiting one weekend soon after we relocated to Mt. Shasta, and during breakfast our daughter-in-law commented about how much she enjoyed the breakfast. She reached in her purse and handed us a clipping from a travel magazine. It was requesting potential Bed and Breakfast owners to consider advertising in a B&B directory.

"You know, folks," Jann said, "as much as you like to entertain and with the fantastic breakfasts you serve, you really ought to think about making your home into a Bed and Breakfast." Since our initial ranch camp idea had not materialized, we hadn't considered alternatives. As we discussed Jann's suggestion later, we became excited. Barbara redecorated the bedrooms. I busied myself with remodeling the basement. We then contacted the lady responsible for the directory and after meeting with her and praying about it, we decided to convert our home into a Bed and Breakfast.

One August day soon afterwards, we were sitting on our deck, visiting with guests. The telephone rang and Barbara went inside to answer it. In a few minutes she returned, a perplexed expression on her face. "I'm not sure what I got us into for tomorrow night," she mused. "We are having newlyweds for guests."

"That's wonderful," I responded. "We've had newlyweds before."

"But that's not all," replied Barbara. "Her name is Erma and his is Blackfoot."

"Well, for heaven's sake, honey, is that his first name or last?"

"I don't know. I was too embarrassed to ask," was Barbara's answer.

"Well, maybe you're right. Perhaps it will be an interesting day," I replied, grinning at our guests.

Earlier in the week we had booked a couple for the next day who owned a Bed and Breakfast in Downey, California. Now, with the Blackfoot reservation, we would have two guest couples.

The Downey guests arrived about mid-afternoon the following day. We welcomed them and were enjoying refreshments on our front deck. We had been visiting for about half an hour when a small car roared into our driveway. There were three occupants. Barbara and I excused ourselves and went to greet the visitors. Out of the driver's side of the car stepped a young lady. She introduced herself as Erma. From the passenger side unfolded a man about six feet, six inches tall, wearing a complete buckskin outfit, with fringe, a full beard and shoulder-length hair. Around his waist was strapped a twelve-inch sheath knife. Erma introduced him as "Blackfoot." As I shook his hand and looked up into his beady eyes, I managed a "How do you do, Blackfoot." The third person was a little gray-haired lady whom Erma introduced as Hazel. "Hazel," explained Erma, "has come with us to check your house for evil spirits before we decide to stay."

Barbara and I exchanged a quick glance. This was definitely a first for Bigfoot!

As we proceeded up the steps, Erma further explained that Hazel was a mutual friend who had married them at two o'clock that morning on the slopes of Mt. Shasta.

Before they went inside, we also were told that Blackfoot had run away from home when he was eleven and had been raised by the Hopi Indians. Erma added that Hazel was playing the role of the Hopi grandmother.

Blackfoot remained outside with our Downey guests and me. Although not Indian, Blackfoot had obviously adopted a modified Indian life-style. He was extremely knowledgeable about Indian lore. His description of his experiences on Mt. Shasta led me to believe that his expertise in outdoor life was above average. He also shared that he was Bigfoot's "keeper," meaning that he was a "Sasquatch" authority for Northern California and Southern Oregon. Something in his manner was perplexing, but I couldn't identify what it was.

"Bigfoot was at our wedding this morning," the big man volunteered. "I called to him and he answered. I also smelled him."

With that statement our guests' eyes suddenly resembled saucers. I had been holding my own up to now, but that statement threw me, too. I suddenly found myself as enchanted as they were. For an instant I wondered if they thought that these guests were typical of our Bed and Breakfast visitors.

Regaining my composure, I asked Blackfoot when Bigfoot had last been seen in this area. He told us that the previous summer a man was driving south on Interstate 5 from Grants Pass, Oregon. "He looked out of his window," he explained, "and Bigfoot was running parallel to his car."

"Is that right?" I replied, trying desperately to conceal a guffaw. The sudden thought that some people believe in Bigfoot the way others believe in Unidentified Flying Objects helped me to suppress my astonishment.

The front door opened. The ladies had finished the inspection tour.

"Oh," smiled Hazel, "the children will be very safe here. It is delightful!"

Barbara and I stole a quick glance at each other. I felt her silent sigh along with mine. For a split second, I had a revelation. . .

"Certified. . . no evil spirits herein."

Maybe we should insert that statement into our B&B brochure.

By now everyone was hungry. The guests headed into town for dinner. We weren't sure whether the Downey guests would return that evening. They did.

We take pride in our Bigfoot breakfasts. One of our specialties is aebleskivers, a Danish pancake. A typical menu includes coffee, fruit juice, fresh fruit, eggs, bacon, and aebleskivers. Women can eat three or four, men five or six. Blackfoot consumed fifteen. That record still stands! When we began serving and Barbara set the aebleskivers in front of Blackfoot, he shouted delightfully, "Boy, do you ring my bell with those!" He was Danish and his grandmother used to make them for him. He hadn't eaten any for years. It was Sunday and Barbara and I were planning to attend our eleven o'clock church service. At about 10:15 our Downey guests departed. Blackfoot was still eating. As he was finishing, Erma mentioned that they were planning to bake a wedding cake for their reception on the mountain later that day.

"Where are you going to bake your cake?" asked Barbara.

"I really don't know," replied Erma. "We're going to have to find a place."

Then, to my consternation, my obliging wife offered our kitchen. I could not believe my ears. Normally, I would have been all for it, but I was uneasy about Blackfoot. In my mind, his credibility was suspect. Blackfoot and Erma, however, were ecstatic. I quickly (and as inconspicuously as possible) escorted Barbara to our bedroom.

"Honey, aren't we going to church?" I asked. "Surely, you can't be serious about letting them use our kitchen."

"What are you worried about?" quizzed Barbara.

"Plenty. This guy Blackfoot is a peculiar dude— who knows what he'll try to pull," I answered.

"Oh, stop worrying," said my wife, continuing to primp herself for church.

Realizing that her mind was made up, I began to pray.

"Lord," I prayed. "I am having trouble handling this situation and I need your help. Please make me as big a person as my wife and please do it now!"

When we returned to the kitchen, Erma and Blackfoot had retrieved from their car all the necessary ingredients for their cake. . . flour, salt, sugar, eggs, milk, pans. . . and about twelve of the biggest carrots I had ever seen. When Barbara spied the carrots she handed Erma a small hand grater from the cupboard.

"Oh," said Erma, "using that will take forever. Do you have a food processor?"

That was more than I could take, and I was just about to express my feelings when Barbara pointed to the covered food processor and nodded her head in approval.

When we left for church, the food processor was whining like I had never heard it before. Blackfoot, in the meantime, had turned the oven to "preheat" and was mixing the batter, struggling to keep his beard out of it.

On our way to church, I asked Barbara to please do me a favor.

"Let's not linger after church and gab like we usually do."

"Oh, honey," she advised. "Just relax."

Needless to say, I heard little of the pastor's sermon. Instead, I was praying throughout the service. Barbara told me later that the sermon topic was "Trust!"

My wife did a good job of limiting her visiting after church. I quickly ushered her into the car for the trip home. It was then that she informed me that we had to stop at the Safeway market.

"I'll only be a few minutes," she promised.

Exasperated, I muttered begrudgingly, "No woman ever takes just a few minutes to shop."

She surprised me. What seemed like ten hours was only ten minutes.

As we approached our home, I could see that there was no smoke. That was a relief. We ascended the stairway and entered the kitchen. It was immaculate. The counters were spotless. The food processor was in its original location. Blackfoot and Erma were in the process of icing three cakes. One, they informed us, was for us.

As Erma signed our guest book, I helped Blackfoot load their car. They said good-bye and left in a cloud of dust. As we walked back into the house, I was still in a state of disbelief at the entire weekend experience. I picked up the guest book to read what Erma had written. It read, "The peace and perfect beauty that abound here at the foot of majestic Shasta make the Bigfoot Ranch the most perfect setting for a pair of newlyweds. Thank you both, Barbara and Phil, for your loving grace and for sharing your little piece of heaven with us. We appreciated your hospitality and trust to open your kitchen to us. Give us a call if you ever need some help with caretaking the ranch."

I closed the book, suddenly feeling very small and selfish. I looked at Barbara. Her beautiful eyes glistened and she smiled that gorgeous Brewster smile.

"You know," I said, "it isn't easy living with a perfect woman. You knew exactly what those kids needed, didn't you?"

"Well, honey," was the reply. "I just figured that if we had had a daughter and she was two thousand miles from home on her honeymoon, and someone had offered some little thing like the use of their kitchen, we would have certainly appreciated it."

"You're absolutely right," I sighed. "When am I going to learn not to doubt a woman's intuition?"

That night as I lay in bed, I couldn't help but reflect on the unique events of the weekend. I wondered what other experiences God had planned for Barbara and me here at our Bigfoot Ranch, and marveled at the way our lives had unfolded since our decision to move to the mountains.

In Pursuit of a Dream

Saratoga, California, was a beautiful, serene little village when Barbara and I moved there in 1950. Located about an hour's drive south of San Francisco, it had been a sanctuary for the San Francisco elite before World War II. During our 30 years there we raised four wonderful sons, managed to accrue some home equity, developed a multitude of meaningful and long-lasting friends, and obtained an array of experience in the education profession.

Early in our marriage we had the privilege of counseling at a summer ranch camp on the Northern California coast. It was at Plantation Camp that we observed the positive and long-lasting effects that can result when children have the opportunity to be surrounded by farm animals, an outdoor setting, and caring and loving individuals. We started to dream about having our own ranch camp someday.

In 1975 we began to think seriously about "our dream." Ours sons were on their own, the village of Saratoga had been discovered by thousands of others, and the rapid decline in school enrollment was seriously affecting teacher morale. It seemed like a good time to start looking for a place to retire, and put our savings, plans, and experience into that ranch camp.

We concentrated our search for a suitable ranch setting in Siskiyou County, the northernmost county in California, and the one in which I was born and raised. It offered the type of environment we wanted for our ranch.

After numerous visits to a variety of potential settings, we determined that there was nothing appropriate within our means. We decided that we would continue our search at a somewhat slower pace, place our "dream" in the hands of the Lord, and wait to see what would happen.

Early in 1979 we received a call from one of my real estate friends in Mt. Shasta. She told us that a small ranch close to the city had just been placed on the market. It sounded interesting, so we made an appointment to see it the following weekend. What we found there was to become our future home.

A Dream Come True

As Mary drove us down Hill Road, I remembered that I had been there before. I used to come there in my youth because one of my favorite fishing streams was Wagon Creek. My absence of thirty years, however, had erased the exact details of the area.

The ranch was a nine-acre parcel, situated about two miles from the center of town. The property was surrounded by timber. . . huge cedars, firs, and occasional oaks. As we drove into the driveway we observed a nice appearing, two-story house surrounded on three sides by lawn. It was serene and beautiful! Immediately to the west, running directly through the property, was Wagon Creek.

We walked up the stairway made of railroad ties to the front door. As Mary rang the door bell, Barbara and I turned East. There, in all her beauty, was an unparalleled view of one of the most magnificent works of Nature we had ever seen. . . the lady herself, majestic Mt. Shasta. It seemed close enough to touch.

I had gone to high school with the present owners and we renewed our acquaintance as they showed us their home. It was a well-built, lovely house. It showed immaculate care and, what was even more important, Barbara liked the floor plan.

The property itself was unique, with the features we desired. There were four acres of solid timber, three pastures, and several "out" buildings. . . a barn, a carport, a garden house, a creek, hiking trails, views in every direction, remoteness. . . everything that encompasses a ranch-camp setting.

We left Mary with the understanding that she would hear from us within the week.

As we drove home we realized we had a monumental decision to make. Now that we had found what we had been looking for and dreaming of all these years, were we really ready to "pull up stakes" and move?

The next week was both exciting and discomforting. We realized that the time had come, sooner than we had expected, to decide our future. Did we have the heart to leave Saratoga, our home for 30 years. . . a beautiful house, situated in one of the nicest locations in the city; close, dear friends we loved; and a church family second to none? Was it something we really wanted to do? Would we be happy in Mt. Shasta? Would the snow and cold weather make us yearn for the climatic desirability of the Santa Clara Valley? Could we possibly get by on one retirement income and the corresponding change in life-style? We also realized that because of the escalating real estate market, once we sold our Saratoga home we would be unable to return. We continued to pray and ask God for direction and wisdom. We finally decided that moving would mean "burning our bridges," following our heart, praying for guidance, and in a sense, "gambling" on the future. One thing we knew for sure: we had each other and that was what mattered the most!

Fortunately, during this time of indecision, our sense of humor prevailed. Mt. St. Helens had just erupted and many of our Saratoga friends were mortified that we would consider moving to the foot of a volcano. We shrugged it off nonchalantly by responding that Mt. Shasta hadn't erupted in over 200 years and that it was constantly being monitored. However, our friends' concern did raise our awareness level. Finally, Barbara said to me, "Okay, honey, I'll move to Mt. Shasta, but the first wisp of white smoke I see coming off the mountain, I'm heading back to Saratoga!" I replied, "Now let's think about that for just a minute. Look at it this way. Either we live in Saratoga on the

San Andreas Fault, where there would be no warning and certainly no room to run, or we live at the foot of the volcano where we probably would have sufficient warning and certainly a heck of a lot more running room!" "That's true," was her reply. "I guess you're right!"

It was during this time that we began to think about a name for our ranch. Those indigenous to the Shasta area were taken. As we brainstormed, several possibilities emerged. Barbara suggested "Singing Cedars." We had a good laugh when I responded, "Wait a minute. Here's a young boy who returns home after spending two weeks at our summer camp. Somebody asks him where he went to camp. . . and he replies, 'Thinging Cedars.'"

"You have a point," laughed Barbara. "Maybe Bigfoot would be better after all."

Supposedly, Bigfoot has been sighted in certain areas of Northern California. Because the Sasquatch legend is famous and intriguing, especially to children, we decided that the name "Wards' Bigfoot Ranch" might appeal to potential campers.

By the end of the week, we had reached a decision. We knew that the property in Mt. Shasta would sell quickly. We couldn't delay any longer. That fact, coupled with the all-around desirable attributes which the area offered, helped us to decide that now was the time for action. Bigfoot, here we come!

A New Family Member

Our friends could not believe our decision. "Phil," said one, "you're giving up all this to move to Mt. Shasta. . . why?"

Several others wanted to bet that we would be back within one year. Two or three others agreed, but thought that it might be two years. These comments were not the most encouraging we had ever heard. They added precious little consolation to two people who weren't sure that they had made the right decision in the first place. Nevertheless, we had made it and there was no turning back. . . our house was for sale, we had signed an agreement to purchase the Mt. Shasta property, and I had officially notified my school district of my intention to retire at the end of the school year. The dye was cast!

Shortly thereafter the Saratoga School District decided to eliminate school bus service. One afternoon while talking to the Business Manager, he mentioned that the buses would be appraised soon for public sale. That night, as Barbara and I discussed the day's activities, I casually mentioned the topic. As we talked, the idea of purchasing a bus began to evolve. We could do all kinds of things. . . use it as a moving van, a thought that was not overly popular with Barbara, especially since I had promised that the next time we moved, it would be done "with class;" or, how about field trips for our ranch campers? We reasoned that when and if we established our own educational consulting business, we could convert it into a portable classroom. Properly equipped, it would provide an ideal facility to conduct teacher workshops at "on site" locations.

The next day I talked the Business Manager into letting me take "Number 14" for a quick spin. I was impressed, and by the time the appraisal had been made, we had decided to buy it.

"OK," said Barbara, "Now we need a name for it."

"I've already got one," I replied.

"Really?" responded Barbara. "What?'

"Sheasta," I said.

"Why Sheasta?" quizzed Barbara.

"Well, think about it," I said proudly. "First of all, we're moving to Mt. Shasta. And second, she has to have gas, she has to have oil, and she has to have water. How about that?"

"You're absolutely impossible," she quirked.

"That's true, but what you see is what you get and look at what you've got now. . . not only me, but a new family member, too!"

Onward to Bigfoot

The day of the "big move" arrived. I removed the seats from Sheasta and stored them in a neighbor's attic. That made room in the bus for most of our furniture. Our pickup was fully loaded, as was the small homemade trailer behind it. The only space left in the family Oldsmobile was a tiny spot for a very small driver. It was hooked to a large covered U-Haul trailer. The day before, as we were furiously cramming 30 years of belongings into these vehicles, a sympathetic neighbor graciously offered his pickup for our use.

As the expedition departed from our cul-de-sac home, some neighbors held handkerchiefs to their eyes; others managed a smile and a wave. The lumps in our throats were obvious and I fought to hold back the tears. Barbara didn't!

I drove the bus. Barbara followed in our Ford truck pulling the trailer. Behind her came son Phil, in the Olds pulling the U-Haul. He had talked a friend into driving the borrowed pickup.

Our caravan had travelled about four miles when Barbara began honking furiously behind me. I could see her plainly in the side-view mirror. Something was definitely wrong. I pulled over at the first stop light. Barbara pulled alongside. "The house plants," she yelled, with hair flying. "They're hanging outside the door of the bus!" They had been the last things loaded, and the only space left had been the steps of the bus entrance. I had placed them there as we began our trek, but hadn't noticed I had closed the door on them. I struggled to rearrange them, but before I knew it the traffic light had changed. I had to go. Little did I realize that the rest of the trip would be spent brushing oleandar, veronica, and bottlebrush limbs aside so I could see the highway. I literally felt as though I was leading a safari through the jungle.

Our expedition crossed the San Francisco Bay about an hour later. As I approached the bridge toll gate, I pulled into the adjacent parking lot and walked to the toll house. I wanted to pay the toll for each of our vehicles as they arrived individually. First came Phil; then John. Now, where was Barbara? She had been right behind me the last time I looked. I reflected on what she had said as we left Saratoga, "Now remember, don't go over 45 miles per hour. I haven't ever driven this truck and since I'm pulling a trailer, I don't want to go too fast."

"OK, honey," I had replied. "Don't worry about a thing. Just follow me."

It was about five minutes before I caught a glimpse of the truck and trailer approaching the toll gate. Those five minutes seemed like five hours!

As she approached, it appeared that she was crying.

"What in the world has happened?" I thought. And for a frightful moment my mind played havoc with me. Had she run over someone or something? Was she hurt? What in the world could be wrong?

As she pulled to a stop, I quickly opened the door. She was still crying and her beautiful brown eyes were now red and watery. "You . . . you. . . you said you wouldn't go over 45 and I. . . I couldn't keep up with you! And . . . .and I'm hungry and you haven't stopped for breakfast like you said you would. And besides that," she sobbed, "I don't have any money and I didn't know how I was going to get over this bridge! I want to go back to Saratoga!" All this deluge from that darling wife of mine in a matter of mega-seconds. I felt terrible. How could I have blundered so many times on such an important day? What I didn't know then was that Sheasta's speedometer was unusually marked and when I thought I was going 45, I was really doing 55.

At the very next opportunity, we stopped and had breakfast.

The rest of the trip was uneventful. After all, what could compare with that first hour on the road?

A Safeway Special

We became the official owners of the Mt. Shasta property on August 1, 1980. Since our house in Saratoga had not sold, we decided that we would spend the month of August redecorating our new house. We were excited, and the idea of moving into a newly decorated home was something we had experienced only once before in our marriage. Our anxiety prompted us to begin immediately.

The third of August is Barbara's birthday. Although we had not moved any furniture, we had trailered several odd pieces of outdoor furniture to Mt. Shasta. Included among these was our outdoor barbecue. I thought it would be fun to invite my parents and a few close friends to an informal barbecue to celebrate Barbara's special day.

We gathered on our back patio. The briquettes were heating, the salad and other goodies our parents and friends had brought were carefully in place, and we were all having a wonderful visit. Suddenly I realized I had forgotten the dessert. I graciously excused myself and drove to the Safeway store, about two miles away. As I was about to enter the store, I noticed a young boy sitting outside the entrance. On the ground next to him was a large cardboard box. I glanced inside. There were three of the cutest puppies I had ever seen!

"Golly, what cute pups," I remarked. "Are you selling them?"

"No," the youngster replied, "we have too many dogs at home now and Mom and Dad say I have to get rid of them, so I'm giving them away."

"What kind are they?" I asked.

"They're a mixture of Lasa Apso, Cock-a-Poo, and Poodle," he answered.

I picked one up. He was solid black except for a little splotch of white under his chin. All three were about the size of guinea pigs, and almost as pudgy. I began to think. . . "I don't have Barbara's birthday present yet." Quickly, another thought popped into place. "We have the ranch now. There's plenty of room for a second dog." I couldn't resist. I said to the youngster, "Look, I have to buy something inside but I want that one," and pointed to the pup I had held.

All the way back to the ranch, my little friend snuggled against my shoulder. I was so tickled that I could hardly wait to give him to Barbara. I quickly waltzed up the back steps, the ice cream in one hand and the pup in the other behind my back. When I reached the patio, I set the ice cream down and said to Barbara, "Close your eyes, honey, and hold out your hands." She did. As I gently placed the pup in her palms, she opened her eyes. She was overjoyed. Everyone oohed and aahed at the little guy. He was an instantaneous hit!

We had him about a week before we could think of an appropriate name. We finally decided that he seemed so grateful to be with us and was always so happy that we would name him just that . . . "Happy."

Shortly thereafter Barbara departed for Saratoga. I remained at the ranch to carry on with the painting. The morning after she left, I was just awakening. Suddenly, I heard Happy yelp. He had been sleeping downstairs in the basement with our other dog, Gunner. I quickly dashed down the stairs. There, in a prone position, with eyes open but glazed, motionless, and not breathing, lay the little pup. I immediately saw what had happened. He had chewed the extension cord attached to a borrowed refrigerator and had electrocuted himself! For a split second I was petrified. The sight of that cute little ball of fur, who just the night before had been frolicking with Gunner and me, lay absolutely still. Tears in my eyes, I picked him up. He was as limp as a wet dish rag. I didn't know what to do. I found myself blubbering helplessly, and hugging, petting and talking to him. In my confusion, I did have the presence of mind to ask God for help. "Please, Lord," I think I said, "this little creature can't be dead. What can I do?" A sudden inspiration told me to place him on the bottom step and massage his chest. Vigorously, I did so. Then I picked him up and shook him briskly. . . to no avail. I repeated the process. He started to wag his tail and lick my face. I couldn't believe it. I sat down on the stairs, pressing him close to my bosom and while he was licking, I bawled like a baby. God and I had brought him back to life!

Where's the Beef?

The former owners of our newly-acquired ranch had given permission to a neighbor to graze his cows in our pastures. We thought that was a good idea. The cows were automatic lawnmowers and kept the weeds to a minimum. We lived with that for the first year. But as we analyzed the situation we began to think about how nice it would be to raise our own beef. "You know," Barbara said one day, "we could really be quite self-sufficient. With the nice garden we will have, if we had our own beef, what more could we want?"

"That's not such a bad idea," I replied. "We could save money, too."

The following spring we considered buying a small beef cow. Every week there was a livestock auction yard about 35 miles north. Not knowing "siccum" about cows, I asked my Dad and Uncle Bud if they would go with me and give me the benefit of their experience. Bud was raised on a ranch in Nebraska and Dad had had considerable experience with farm animals during his youth. They were happy to help.

We arrived at the auction yard about an hour early and looked around. I really had come to look at what was available, that's all. I wasn't even sure whether I wanted a cow.

Shortly thereafter, the auction began. The three of us sat watching the proceedings for some time. Finally, two white-faced Angus steers were led into the ring. They must have weighed about 350 pounds each. Bud nudged me in the ribs and said that he thought they would be great. "Do you really think so, Bud?" I replied. "Shore," he quipped. "Go for it!"

I was hesitant, and rather timidly raised a finger at apparently a crucial moment. Suddenly, almost before I realized what had happened, Barbara and I were the owners of not one cow, but two! Now what? There I was, 35 miles from home, with two 350-pound calves, and no way to transport them. What was I going to do?

After inquiring with the auction yard owners, I was told that a fellow in Mt. Shasta often hauled livestock. I readily recognized his name and realized that he was a former high school classmate. I called Roger, who informed me that he would be able to deliver them the following day. "That's great, Roger," I said. "Call me when you have them loaded so I'll know about when to expect you at Bigfoot."

When I arrived home and told Barbara of our new acquisitions, she was surprised. "Two?" she murmured. "I thought we were going to start small."

"So did I," I replied, "but Uncle Bud thought this opportunity was too good to pass up."

The next day Roger arrived with the critters. As he drove through the gate, I noticed that they seemed wild. He drove into our middle pasture. When he removed the end gate of the truck's chute, the first steer jumped out and headed for the north side of the pasture. The second one ejected like a shot out of a gun! Zip! Almost that fast he was through the first fence and headed for the second. Before I knew what had happened, he raced through the last fence and disappeared into our four acres of solid timber. I immediately envisioned dollar bills evaporating spontaneously into the air. Stunned, I said to Roger, "Wow, what do I do now?"

"Well," he drawled, "have you got a horse?"

"Heck no," I countered. "What would I do with one if I had one?"

"Ya better call the Humane Society and let them know you have a lost animal," he suggested. And then, holding out his hand he mumbled, "That'll be twenty-five dollars."

Still in a state of shock, I paid him and off he drove.

Barbara and I searched for the steer the remainder of the day. We even checked adjoining pastures and alerted our neighbors of our plight. All felt sure the animal would return. I had my doubts. Having no additional fencing around our timber area, I envisioned that the animal would be close to the top of Mt. Eddy by then.

The next day we decided we needed more help if we were going to successfully retrieve the lost animal. The local radio station provides a daily announcement service. For ten dollars, they make five announcements during the day. I called the station.

"Sure, Phil, we'll be glad to help you," was the response. "Now describe the steer, please."

"Heck," I retorted, "I didn't seem him long enough to know what he looks like. I do know that he's black with a white face and weighs about 350 pounds."

Later that day the first announcement was broadcast. "Ladies and gentlemen," said the voice, "Phil Ward needs your help. He lost a steer two days ago in the vicinity of Hill Road. He thinks it's black and white. If you see a young steer answering this description, or anything close to it, please call him."

That evening, we returned home after visiting friends. There was a message on our code-a-phone. People in our small community are not used to a taped telephone response. My neighbor's message graphically illustrated that point.

"Phil," my neighbor sighed, "This is. . . eh. . . eh. .
. Joe. . . Joe Lombardi. Call me when you get home!" A
sudden click at the end of the message indicated that
he couldn't wait to get off the phone. Due to the late-
ness of the hour, I decided to call him the next morning.

When I called, Joe informed me that our calf had
appeared at his ranch.

"I heard my cows bawling about dusk last night
and went out to see what was causing it," he explained.
"Your calf was on the other side of the fence trying to
get in. I opened the gate to let him in, but instead of
going through the gate, he went over it. Phil, I think
you should know that you have a wild animal on your
hands!" Joe ended the conversation by volunteering to
return the calf the next day.

Early the next morning I reinforced our fences. Dad
and Uncle Bud, who by this time had become grossly
involved in our cattle raising experience, were quick to
volunteer assistance. In a short time we had reworked
the fences and I felt secure.

When Joe returned the steer, we were ready. Dad
was on the west boundary of the pasture, Uncle Bud on
the east. I had stationed myself at the exact spot where
the animal had exited previously. I had my cowboy hat
on and was holding a lariat. In retrospect, I had no idea
what I would do with it, but at the time, it seemed appropriate for all of the right reasons. Meanwhile, Bar-

bara had positioned herself on the deck in front of our house waiting for the show to begin. As Joe opened the tailgate, out flew the little steer. He headed straight for his previous point of exit. This time, however, I was there to meet him. As he stormed my way, I yelled and waved my rope. That worked and he started to run parallel to the fence. When he got to the gate, he futilely tried to climb it. Sensing that he could not escape, he backed away and quieted down.

As we sat on the back patio rehashing our experience, Uncle Bud opined that our two steers probably had never seen anyone except on horseback and had probably been born and raised in a remote area. "Furthermore," theorized Bud, "they were probably drugged just before the auction." That hypothesis made sense to me.

During the next five months the animals adapted to their new environment fairly well, although some elements of wildness were still evident. We could see that their weight was increasing and our aspirations for home-grown beef heightened.

One morning in November, I noticed that the wild one was hesitant to eat. That was unusual. Upon closer observation, I could see that his entire lower jaw and throat were filled with porcupine quills. No wonder he showed little interest in food. What should I do? How could I help this poor animal? Perplexed, I began to brainstorm ideas of how I could extract the quills. I called the local veterinarian and asked him if he had a tranquilizer gun. He did not. Eventually, I devised what I thought was a brilliant scheme. I would again enlist the help of my Dad and together, we would solve the problem. My final strategy was simple: I would tie a rope around the tree next to the feed trough, and then place a loop over the trough itself. When the animal began to eat, I would put the loop tightly around the neck of the wild one. When he was secured, I would put a second rope around his neck. Dad would then hold it steady and while the tree anchored the other rope, I would extract the quills using pliers. Considering my lack of experience with such things, I was quite proud of this plan. Dad thought the idea was feasible and readily agreed to help.

Early Saturday morning everything was in order. The rope was around the tree, the loop was over the trough, and the extra rope was in place. I had a strong pair of pliers in my pocket. As the cows approached, I anxiously awaited the precise moment. Just at what appeared to be the right time I yanked the rope. To this day, I don't know what went wrong, but the loop pulled taut on the wrong cow. When this happened the wild one quickly departed. The remaining animal became furious. Try as I might I could not free the rope. In my attempt to untie the knot, I was caught between the tree and the cow and almost cut in half! Dad finally cut my brand new rope to free me.

Having failed miserably, I decided to call the local vet again for advice. "When cows on the open range are 'quilled,'" he explained, "the quills usually fester and fall out." He cautioned that I should keep a close eye on the animal to observe his eating habits. He advised that if the animal continued to show signs of not eating, we should accelerate our butchering date. During the next couple of days he appeared to eat normally.

One morning, about two weeks later, when I went to feed our beef, the wild one was laying down. That was most unusual. He was totally disinterested in food or water. Realizing that this was serious, I again called the local vet. He was on vacation and unavailable. Bewildered and confused, I called the vet in Yreka. The nurse informed me that both vets were in consultation and could not come to the phone. "Perhaps I can help you," she suggested. "What seems to be the matter?"

"I have a sick cow," I replied.

"Well," was her response, "have you taken its temperature?"

"I beg your pardon," I stammered. "Do. . . do. . . do you mean a rectal type of temperature?"

"Why, yes," was the reply.

That threw me for a complete loop. After all, she was talking to a novice. She didn't know that at the time, but I did! Quickly pulling myself together, I muttered something including my thanks and hung up.

I was perplexed and frustrated. What does one do when a cow is sick and no professional advice is available? To add to my dilemma was the fact that I was due momentarily for an appointment in Yreka. Suddenly I remembered my old friend and neighbor, Joe Lombardi. After all, wasn't he as familiar with the wild one as I was? Besides, he was an experienced rancher, owned 200 head of cattle, and always seemed ready, willing, and able to help. I raced to his ranch to find him. I was told he was somewhere in town. I finally found him visiting with the guys in the local fire house. I told him my plight. "I can't get out to your place until noon," he told me, "but I'll go by then and give him a shot of penicillin."

"That would be much appreciated, Joe," I said gratefully and quickly headed for Yreka.

That evening I returned home after dark. I quickly changed clothes, grabbed a flashlight, and headed for the south pasture. I had high hopes of finding our steer in better condition than when I left. Unfortunately, such was not the case. I found him in the middle of the pasture, dead and frozen stiff. Chagrined, I went inside and called Joe. He told me that by the time he arrived the animal was beyond help. He also revealed the disheartening news that since the cause of death was undetermined, the meat was lost. I couldn't believe it! I then asked him how one goes about disposing of a carcass. He told me of a tallow company in Oregon and gave me their telephone number. The next morning I called.

"I'm so sorry," said the receptionist. "Our truck was in Mt. Shasta yesterday and only goes down there once each week. However, one of our trucks will be in Yreka tomorrow and if you are willing to pay for the gas the driver will come down there." And then she added, "But he will not pick up the cow in the pasture. It will have to be in your driveway."

The next morning I backed our four-wheel-drive truck to the location of the dead cow. Jumping out I suddenly realized that I had never had to tow a carcass before. "Where do I start?" I pondered. "Do I attach a rope to the horns, the tail, or what?" Apparently the good Lord was smiling down on me, for I suddenly realized that the most substantial and logical part of the body to attach the rope to was the rear hoofs. Looping the rope around the trailer hitch of the truck, I placed it in four-wheel-drive and slowly pulled the dead animal to the front of our home. I was very glad that Barbara was not home. The sight of that cow being pulled behind our truck, burrowing a six-inch furrow in our driveway probably would have been grossly distasteful to her.

After depositing the beast at the end of the driveway in front of our home, I anxiously awaited the arrival of the tallow truck. Somehow the sight of that frozen carcass in front of our home, lying there with all four legs stiffly upright made for something less than a desirable sight.

Occasionally, friends who have not heard of this experience suggest that we should try raising our own beef. Barbara and I steal a quick glance at each other and smile, endeavoring to respond as politely as possible. What these friends don't know is that the one time we tried it, our meat ended up costing us about twelve dollars a pound. And we wanted to be self-sufficient!

Well, "Hello," Tom!

One September afternoon shortly after arriving in Mt. Shasta, Barbara and I were taking a lunch break, visiting and relaxing on our back patio. A car slowly meandered into our driveway. Up the steps came John and LuAnne Boswell, close friends from Saratoga and our first out-of-town visitors. They were returning from John's college class reunion in Seattle. As we exchanged greetings we noticed that John was carrying a large cardboard box. "We wanted to bring you a housewarming present," LuAnne said, "and we've searched this county over." Precisely at that moment a young turkey poked his head out of the box! John quickly disappeared and returned with a fifty-pound sack of poultry feed. "There," he smiled proudly. "You can feed him well and by Thanksgiving you'll have enough turkey for both you and your sons."

Little did we realize that this "acquisition" was soon to become a memorable part of our lives.

The bird was with us about a week before we named him. "Why don't we call him Tom?" suggested Barbara. "Fine," I replied. "What an unusual name!"

He adapted to his new environment quickly. Before we realized it, he had endeared himself to us. He was becoming immense; I began to wonder if maybe there wouldn't be enough Thanksgiving turkey to feed all of our Mt. Shasta relatives.

As Thanksgiving Day drew near, Barbara said to me, "You know, honey, I don't think I can eat Tom."

"I feel the same way," I replied.

The holidays passed and Tom remained, firmly entrenched in his surroundings.

Our friends and guests began to look forward to seeing Tom. Somehow, the idea of a pet turkey was unique and people found it fascinating. We would often receive thank-you notes and postcards from guests with the salutation, "Dear Barbara, Phil, and Tom."

Numerous Saratoga friends journeyed to Mt. Shasta to visit us that first year. They were enchanted with the surroundings and the beauty of the area. Large cedars, firs, and oaks give one the feeling of complete isolation and serenity. Wagon Creek meanders through this paradise, and the view through the fir boughs is breathtaking.

A popular activity for visitors was to take a stroll through our four acres of timber. When they did, I would lead, followed by our friends, then our dogs and cats, and finally, Barbara. It was a safari that our "flat land" friends truly enjoyed. Tom was an integral part of the activity. He would usually follow Barbara, lagging about ten yards behind the troop. If we got too far ahead, he would gobble. The whole contingent would have to stop and wait for him to catch up. The sight of that turkey trying to maintain his position in the lineup as he hurdled fallen logs was hilarious. That experience definitely added to his reputation.

A favorite hangout for Tom was within the fenced area that leads to our south pasture. It was a strategic location because from there he commanded a view of the arrival of all visitors. When a car would drive in, he would start to gobble until he received the attention he felt he deserved. Guests usually had one of two reactions. They might remark something like, "I've never seen such an ugly bird up so close."

"Please don't say that to his face," I might reply. "After all, he has feelings, too."

Others might express the desire to stroke him. I would then open the gate, pick him up, and watch him relish the attention.

Tom's domain was behind the barn. On one occasion, shortly after his arrival, I went out to feed him. I then jogged back to the house. In my haste to say something to Barbara, I forgot to close the sliding glass door. Barbara motioned for me to look. Tom had followed me directly into the house. I quickly herded him out with the threat that if he was going to make a habit of intruding, he would soon end up in the stew.

Tom survived his second Thanksgiving, but was becoming more aggressive with age. One day both Barbara and I were working around the barn. "It's time to feed Tom," I said. "I'll go fill his trough while you herd him back there." I proceeded and waited for Barbara and Tom to arrive. I waited. After a reasonable time, I yelled, "Are you coming?"

"Tom won't follow me," was the answer.

"Pick up a branch and prod him," I advised. "Then he'll come."

Still no Barbara. Somewhat exasperated, I sauntered around the corner of the barn. There stood Barbara, stick in hand, prodding the bird. The only thing wrong was that Barbara was retreating and Tom was stalking her.

Later I told her that Tom really had her "buffaloed."

"Not true," she smiled, "he has me 'turkeyoed'."

One day, in the spring of Tom's third year with us, we noticed that Tom had not eaten his food. We knew something was awry. We began searching. We had ventured only a few yards from the barn when we found his remains. Coyotes, rather than a Thanksgiving feast, had terminated his memorable stay at Bigfoot.

TON-DE-LAY-O

I read that the Bureau of Land Management of the Federal Government occasionally offered wild horses and mules to the public for adoption. Since we now owned a ranch, we decided that our grandchildren should certainly have a horse or donkey to ride when they came to visit Grandma and Granddad. I contacted the Bureau and was advised that some animals were going to be available in the near future. I mentioned this to a friend. He happened to know a lady who had a donkey for sale. I contacted her. "He is a tame, ride-able animal about three years old," she told me, "and his name is Jasper. I'll sell him cheap. He is out at our ranch. If you want to, you can drive out and see him." The next day was rainy and cold. I drove to her ranch. As I approached the pasture, Jasper was nowhere in sight. There was, however, a barn nearby. Jasper's owner had said that he would probably be inside. "Jasper, are you there?" I yelled. No Jasper. But from around the corner of the barn appeared the head of a horse.

"Hey, where's Jasper?" I smirked, halfway laughing. Still no Jasper. Then suddenly, as if by magic, Jasper's long ears appeared below the horse's head. "Well, hello. Come over here Jasper," I hollered. Somewhat hesitantly, he started toward me. Then he stopped abruptly, apparently sensing that I was a stranger. I observed a rather small, winter-coated, grey burro. As he stood there surveying me, his ears stood upright like two grey smokestacks. I could imagine what he was thinking. "Who is this character? Do I like him or not?"

Something about him tickled me. I began to laugh. "How would you like to come to Bigfoot?" I asked. He didn't bat an eye. As he stood there I envisioned him hauling the children around our pasture. They would be thrilled. "Jasper, I think you're it," I said and then and there decided to buy him.

The morning after Jasper arrived at our ranch, I arose early to feed him. The pasture gate had been mauled and pushed open. Jasper was nowhere to be found! After checking all three pastures it was evident that he had left the premises.

"Barbara!" I screamed. "Come here quick!"

Being rather used to my frantic antics, Barbara quickly appeared, grabbed a rope, and pointed to the pickup. Off we went. When we reached the main road, we stopped. "Which way?" I queried.

"I don't know," she answered, "why not try north?"

About one hundred yards up the road we spotted Jasper. A neighbor, realizing that the animal belonged to someone, was trying to lure him with a handful of hay. The passing parade of cars at this time in the morning, however, hindered his efforts. Barbara quickly jumped out to help. When I saw that the little animal was in a frenzy, I yelled that I would go back and get his feed bucket. I drove to the ranch, grabbed the bucket, and headed back down the road. I hadn't gone a hundred yards when Jasper appeared with Barbara in hot pursuit, smiling triumphantly. Overjoyed, I jumped out of the truck with feed bucket in hand. At that instant, Jasper saw me and whirling quickly, galloped back past Barbara, disappearing behind her. My little donkey-herder was livid.

"Why did you do that?" she screamed. "I had him headed for home and you. . . you. . . " She didn't need to finish. The frustration and anguish in her voice said it all.

"Oh, you dope, Phil, what have you done?" I thought to myself.

Barbara jumped in the truck again and once more, we sped off. In the distance we spied Jasper at a nearby intersection. He had headed in another direction this time, but again, a good samaritan had headed him off in his pickup. Quickly and deliberately, Barbara jumped out of the truck and hid behind a nearby bush. This time my truck and I headed hell-bent for election, in the opposite direction. I wasn't about to pull the same stupid trick a second time.

Our combination of endeavors worked. Jasper again headed for home with Barbara following. I didn't reappear until she had corralled the donkey and secured all gates.

Since owning a donkey was a new experience for both of us, we were constantly seeking suggestions from our more experienced friends about proper ways to care for a burro. One day, one of my former high school classmates and her husband dropped by for a visit. He was an experienced horseman. During the visit he mentioned to Barbara that a good way to make friends with Jasper was to feed him tobacco.

"Just buy some cigarettes, crumple them, and feed them to Jasper once or twice a day," suggested Burt. "In no time he will treat you like you were the best friend he ever had."

We took his advice. Barbara bought several packages of cigarettes and twice a day she would feed the tobacco to our new acquisition. It was a great idea and Jasper cooperated beautifully. When she was finished feeding him, she would put the opened package of cigarettes on top of the holding tank in the pump house where they would be handy the next time she came out to feed Jasper.

Shortly thereafter, a couple who had gone to college with us dropped by. I hadn't seen Dutch in ten years and neither he nor his wife had visited us at our ranch. As I was showing Dutch around the property he expressed an interest in our well. I explained that we had a holding tank and pointed to where it was housed in the well-house. He wanted to see what a well-house looked like. I was happy to show him. I opened the door and explained the setup to my friend. As I was busy showing him, he happened to see the opened package of cigarettes on top of the holding tank.

"For Pete's sake, Phil," questioned Dutch, "do you have to come out here to smoke?"

I laughed and said, "Oh, I don't smoke, Dutch. Barbara has those out here for our donkey."

"Donkey?" queried Dutch. "You must be putting me on!"

When I explained how we had discovered that our donkey liked tobacco and how friendly he had become as a result, Dutch was amazed. I'm sure that at the moment, he felt I was really pulling his leg.

Later that day, the four of us were sitting on our deck, having refreshments and reminiscing. I noticed that Jasper was heading for his favorite spot to roll in the dirt. I had observed this behavior on previous occasions and thought I could predict when it would happen. Sure enough, my timing was perfect. When the time was right, I yelled, "Hey, Jasper, roll over for our friends." I held my breath. At that instant he dropped to his knees, plopped himself on his backside, and began smothering himself with dirt. Our guests were awestruck.

"Did. . . did. . . did you teach that donkey to roll over?" said Dutch.

"Yes," l smiled, "but it wasn't easy. Must have taken me about two weeks to teach the little dickens how to do that."

The following summer, we were visited by a family of six. The oldest daughter was a senior in veterinary school. About fifteen minutes after their arrival, she and her sister had made friends with Jasper and were riding him, having the time of their lives. So was Jasper!

About a week after this incident, our youngest son, Mike, came home from college. We hadn't seen him since the previous Christmas and we had a lot to talk about. During our initial conversation Barbara casually mentioned how much fun the visitors had riding Jasper. When Mike heard the girls had ridden him, he was amazed. He had tried his luck riding Jasper on previous occasions and had always failed miserably. Mike is by nature a most competitive young man and the thought of girls being successful riding Jasper when he hadn't apparently bothered him more than we realized.

The following day, he was removing some fence posts from our garden area. The thought of the girls riding the burro finally got the best of him. When his work was finished he went to the pump house, grabbed Jasper's halter rope, and opened the pasture gate. Now Mike is a fine young man. . . an excellent athlete, and strong, quick, and agile. But somewhere along the line I failed to teach him how to approach donkeys. His idea of catching Jasper was to make a beeline for him, with rope in hand, simultaneously yelling at him to "Come here!" That might work with some animals, but it didn't work with Jasper.

Soon thereafter, Mike entered the house. "Mom," he volunteered in a subdued tone, "I had a little dis-agreement with Jasper and his neck is badly cut."

In his effort to catch Jasper, Mike had chased Jas-per into the barbed wire fence surrounding the pasture and severely lacerated his neck. When Barbara checked the damage it was evident that medical attention was necessary. The local veterinarian arrived later that day. In order to suture the gaping neck wound, it was neces-sary to place a large clamp on Jasper's nose. "This serves two purposes," he explained to Barbara. "It not only keeps him from reaching around me while I am working on him, but it also helps to momentarily di-vert his concern about his injury."

It was at this time that the vet asked Barbara to hold the clamp to help subdue the animal. Barbara was about a foot from Jasper during this time. Gazing into his cute eyes and sensing the discomfort our little pet was experiencing, and in an effort to console him, she began singing to him. "My donkey walks, my donkey talks, my donkey eats with a knife and fork," warbled Barbara. "Ton-de-lay-o," she continued. But Jasper's discomfort continued. Finally, she thought she had better change tunes. When she began singing "How Great Thou Art" he immediately relaxed.

Dr. Miller suddenly stopped and looked up at Barbara. "Does Jasper like you to sing to him?" he asked. And looking him squarely in the eye, Barbara replied, "Well, he hasn't complained yet."

"OK, Barbara," replied the doctor, "from now on, I'm taking you with me on all my calls."

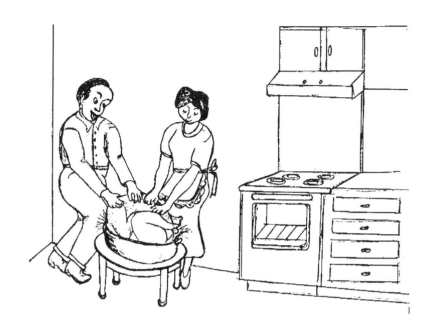

Gobble-Y-Gook

One spring day I was driving home from work and stopped at a feed and poultry store to buy feed for Jasper. I enjoyed this place because it reminded me of an old-fashioned department store. (It also brings back memories of when my brother worked in such a store and the time he lured me into smelling the candy jar he was cleaning with ammonia. He asked me to smell it—I took a big whiff and ended up on the seat of my pants.) The shelves are stocked with Western-style hats and boots. A variety of garden accessories line the aisles. There is always some kind of animal or poultry in the cage near the door. This day was no exception. A shipment of two-day-old turkeys were chirping loudly as I entered. They immediately caught my eye. Ben, the owner, informed me that they were 75 cents apiece and "going fast." The thought entered my mind that it would be fun to raise one for us and one for my folks for Thanksgiving. So I bought two. When I arrived home, Barbara was anything but overjoyed. "Shades of Tom," she sighed. "Will history repeat itself?"

"Oh, no," said I. "We won't name them this time."

For three weeks I kept them in a large cardboard box in our pump house. They flourished! Finally, I decided that they were ready to be placed in the outdoor pen.

Weeks passed and the turkeys grew. In due time we were able to determine that one was a tom, the other a hen.

About two weeks before Thanksgiving I mentioned to Barbara that it would be time to butcher shortly. "But those birds are so big that I'm going to need some help," I said to Barbara.

"I'm not looking forward to that," she responded, "but I will help you."

The turkey feed was depleted by the following Sunday morning so we decided that we would do what had to be done after church. In my inimitable way, I had given careful thought as to how we should proceed. I had been told that one of the steps in the turkey butchering procedure was to secure the wings of the birds so that they wouldn't be able to use them for protection. That sounded logical. I cut two sturdy pieces of rope in preparation for the task.

After church, we came home and changed clothes. I explained my strategy to my cohort. "First, we'll need some hot water," I advised.

"Why not drain the hot water heater?" suggested my fellow butcher.

"That's a great idea," I retorted. "But do we have a vessel large enough to put the turkeys in to scald them?"

"Why can't we use the double boiler that we keep our wood in?"

"That's your second brilliant idea," I raved.

So while Barbara emptied the wood box, I went downstairs to connect a hose to the water heater. The hose lead to the garage. Paper had been placed on the floor. Everything was in order.

"OK, let's go. You take this rope, honey, and quickly tie this rope around his wings when I say to."

We moved quickly. I stalked the biggest bird and finally cornered him. With one hand I held his body. With the other I grabbed him by the throat. He was tremendously strong and wiry; it was all I could do to hold him. "Quick," I stammered. "Now!"

She was Johnny-on-the-spot. Feverishly, she wrapped the cord around the body. It seemed to take forever. Finally, with a quick tug, she cinched it tight. As she did I felt my leg entrapped in the rope.

"For Pete's sake," I shrieked, "you've got my leg tied up. If this bird gets loose, I'll go with him!"

"Oh. . . oh. . . oh," she stammered. "I've got to get my gloves off. I can't untie this knot."

"To heck with the gloves," I hollered. "Get this rope untied."

I suddenly noticed that the turkey wasn't struggling any more. During the struggle I had squeezed his throat so tight that I had cut off his air supply and didn't even know it. I had strangled him. That simplified the procedure used on the hen.

We finally had both birds ready for scalding and subsequent plucking. "There, now that's done. Let's go get the water ready," I said smugly.

While Barbara held the hose, I crawled into the hot water tank storage area where I had connected the hose. Being a new water heater, it didn't have a conventional faucet. Instead, I had to unscrew the spigot to get water. In my excitement, I unscrewed it too far and water began gushing all over me. Try as I might, I couldn't get the pipe threads to match. I yelled to Barbara, panic-stricken. I envisioned water flooding our basement office and inundating the carpeted room. Barbara, thinking I meant to turn off the electrical switch, turned off all the lights. There I was, trying to replace the spigot in total darkness and getting soaked in the process. Finally, the threads engaged. My persistence had paid off.

When I climbed out of the cubby hole, I was soaked from head to foot. To make matters worse, water had leaked from the double boiler all over the garage floor. We hadn't detected the hole. What a mess! We finally managed to heat enough water to finish the job.

That night, we fell into bed, exhausted. We quickly reviewed the day's events and giggled so hard that the bed shook. Finally, I dozed off. I was almost asleep when Barbara murmured, "We have 55 pounds of turkey, don't we? And how many bags of feed did you say it took to feed those birds?"

Sleepily, and somewhat agitated, I replied, "Six, I think."

"And how much was each bag?" she continued.

"Nine dollars."

"Let's see now," she mused. "Fifty-five pounds of turkey and we paid fifty-four dollars plus all the time we spent feeding and butchering. That's easily over a dollar a pound. That makes those thirty-five-cent-a-pound turkeys at Safeway look pretty good, doesn't it?"

We both became hysterical. We laughed so hard that this time the bed didn't just shake, it broke!

The Eleazar Expedition

Our immediate neighbors raise llamas. One of the features of our Bed and Breakfast is our proximity to Jack and Dee Meyer's Alpine Llama Ranch. They have a beautiful ranch and have spent endless hours improving their acreage. When guests express a desire to see their ranch, we take them on a tour. The tour is extremely popular.

We first met the Meyers when both couples moved to Mt. Shasta. It was our suggestion that convinced them to raise llamas. We have been impressed with their dedication and loyalty to their business, and a close friendship has developed.

One June, a baby llama was prematurely born at their ranch. After caring for it night and day for two weeks, they realized that it required more intensive care than they were able to provide. They heard about a lady near Bend, Oregon, who specialized in caring for baby llamas. Her nickname was "the Llama Mama." They took Eleazar to her.

During the summer his health improved, and in September we received an early morning telephone call. It was Dee.

"Hello, Phil," she began. "Please get Barbara on the phone. We want to talk to both of you."

We listened as Dee continued. "Jack and I want you both to plan to go to Bend with us next weekend because Eleazar is ready to come home. Eleazar is a Hebrew name and means 'Whom God has helped,'" she explained. "God has nurtured him back to health, and we want him to meet his new parents."

"I'm afraid I don't understand what you're telling us, Dee," I said.

"Well, we want to give Eleazar to you. We know how much you love llamas, and he would have a wonderful home at the Bigfoot Ranch." she continued. "But there are some strings attached. First, he's still on the bottle and spoiled rotten. You'd have to really discipline him!"

"We've raised four sons, Dee," said Barbara. "We should be able to handle a llama."

"Also," she continued, "somehow his right hind leg keeps popping in and out at the knee socket. We don't know whether it is a result of an injury or his premature development. That will have to be watched very closely."

We assured her that we were willing to undertake that responsibility.

When we hung up, we were thrilled. We had always admired llamas but their cost was prohibitive. The prospect of a baby llama at our ranch was exciting. One week later we headed for Bend in the Meyers' carryall. It was a beautiful Indian summer day. As we journeyed along Highway 97, the conversation centered around Eleazar and the experiences we were going to have with a little boy in the family. We talked about how Jasper might react. We also hypothesized how Eleazar would react to Jasper. And since we knew he would still be "on the bottle," we discussed that.

"Don't worry," smiled Dee. "We have plenty of Pampers at home and you can 'pamper' him and feed him in the house."

"Are you kidding?" replied Barbara, and as she did, we exchanged quizzical looks, coupled with a nervous giggle. I'm sure we both had the same thought: "My gosh, what are we getting ourselves into?"

About halfway to Bend, the excitement erupted within me. The prospect of having a baby llama prompted me to spontaneously roll down the back window and yell, "We're coming, Eleazar. We're coming!"

We arrived at our destination late that afternoon. Sharon and Harv, her husband, were expecting us. So were the thirty-five babies. As we approached the pasture gate we were enthusiastically greeted by seventy scrutinizing eyes. These little camelids resembled a huge litter of puppies. Having been bottle fed since birth, they ran to us, nuzzling with their noses, rubbing with their woolly bodies, and vying for attention. In no time, we found ourselves completely surrounded. I felt as though I'd entered a kindergarten with an armful of cotton candy. And there, in the middle of all this commotion, peeked Eleazar. Dee spotted him instantly and reacquainted herself with him by rubbing noses. He was a handsome little guy, cinnamon in color with a splotch of white spilling over his eyes, down his nose, and around his mouth.

As we looked around, completely enamored with the setting, Jack noticed a regal-looking, young llama a short distance away.

"Gosh, he's a nice looking animal," admired Jack. "Just look at the way he carries himself."

I couldn't help but concur, and during the next hour I quietly observed him. Sharon told me his name was Bobbin, and he truly was a beaut!

That night we stayed in Bend. We meandered around the shopping mall. There Dee spied some stuffed llamas made by an artist who specialized in creating the adorable creatures. She bought two.

When we retired, Barbara and I discussed the possibility of purchasing Bobbin. We had not budgeted for it, but we reasoned that Eleazar was going to need more familiar company than Jasper. We prayed about it and then went to sleep.

The next morning we drove to the magnificent Patterson llama ranch in Sisters, Oregon. It is the largest on the North American continent. As we observed hundreds of llamas peacefully grazing in the pastures it reinforced our appreciation for their beauty and gracefulness.

By the time we returned to pick up Eleazar, we had decided to purchase Bobbin. Jack and Dee shared our excitement.

We left with Bobbin in the back of the carryall and Eleazar kneeling on the floor directly in front of Barbara and me. We had travelled about four miles when Bobbin tired of his solitary confinement status and decided to relocate. He leaped over the back seat directly onto my lap. What a sight we were! Four adults, two live llamas, and two stuffed llamas looking out the back window, heading south on U.S. 97 in a carryall. From the looks we received from fellow travelers, I'm sure the expedition created untold curiosity.

We stopped three times to allow our passengers to stretch. It was like travelling with two good-sized, well-behaved dogs.

When we arrived at the Meyers' ranch, the veterinarian was there to x-ray Eleazar's leg. When he finished, we took the two animals home.

Jasper was livid. What were these two "unknowns" doing in his domain?

For the next two weeks he was unneighborly and obnoxious. When he finally realized that they were here to stay, he began to calm down. In two months, the three of them had become bosom buddies. Jasper began to think and act like a llama. He observed the compliments, handfeeding and petting his friends received, and apparently decided they had a pretty good deal. I periodically remind him that llamas don't have ears as long as his and that his eyelashes are far too short!

A Llama in Room 7

Two weeks had passed since Dr. Miller had x-rayed
Eleazar's leg. Then one day he called to inform us that
the problem appeared to be an injury to the knee joint.
Because he was not familiar with the bone structure of
llamas, he suggested sending the x-ray pictures to a
specialist in Sacramento. We assured him that would
be fine.

It was not very long until we received a call from
Sacramento. Dr. Wharton introduced himself and said
that he had received the pictures.

"We have a saying in veterinary medicine," stated Dr. Wharton. "We like to treat the patient instead of a picture. I really need to see Eleazar in action," he said. "Could you possibly bring him here?"

"We will make it a point to, Doctor," I responded, "just as soon as we can."

When the Meyers heard this they volunteered to take Eleazar. They were going to take one of their female alpacas to the U.C. Davis experimental animal laboratory the next week and were more than happy to help us.

The morning they were scheduled to leave I took Eleazar to meet them. We put both animals in the back of their carryall and they took off. On their drive south, the female alpaca would have nothing to do with Eleazar. She ignored him completely. This apparently agitated him so that he became quite naughty. He reached over and began to chew on Dee's collar. When she censored him, he would momentarily quiet down and then try something else. When they had travelled about two hours, Jack and Dee decided to stop for some breakfast. Returning to their vehicle after eating, Dee noticed a portion of the curtain tie that holds the curtains in their carryall hanging out of Eleazar's mouth. She began to pull. She pulled and pulled, finally extracting the full-length tie with no residual damage to either animal or cloth.

When they arrived at the animal hospital, the alpaca would not exit the carryall unless Eleazar did, too. Consequently, Jack and Dee took both into the building. After some time, it was determined that the alpaca would have to remain at the hospital. Eleazar was led back to the vehicle.

A short time later, they reached Dr. Wharton's office. Dee is a capable and enthusiastic seamstress and has made little coats for the young llamas to wear when they are exposed to cold weather. She reasoned that since neither the doctor nor his staff had ever seen a young llama, she would make sure that their first viewing would be a memorable one. She had prepared accordingly, and before leading Eleazar into the office, she and Jack had dressed him regally. There were colorful tassels hanging from his halter, a bright bandana tied loosely around his neck, and a pleated, hand-stitched jacket covering his body. As they lead the little, long-eyelashed cutie into the reception room, the first person they encountered was the receptionist. Eleazar promptly placed his chin on her desk and looked up at her with his large, brown eyes. She melted! Her screams of delight soon brought the doctor and his assistants running to see what was causing the commotion. For the next twenty minutes Eleazar was the center of attention. When the doctor examined him, he was pleasantly surprised. He told the Meyers that he felt the leg would take care of itself in due time. "If it doesn't," he stated, "have the Wards contact me and we will see what needs to be done."

When Jack and Dee started for home it was quite late. They decided to stay at a motel that evening. When Jack registered, he asked the manager if it would be permissible for Eleazar to stay in their room. Jack explained that the animal was well-behaved and that there would be no problem. "OK," said the manager. "It's an unusual request but we'll take a chance." As Jack left the office, the manager wrote in parentheses in the guest book opposite the Meyers' name, "Llama in Room 7."

Jack, Dee, and Eleazar went to the room. Before retiring, Jack put Eleazar in the bathroom. For the next hour Eleazar caused a minor fracas. He jiggled the toilet seat, walked in the bathtub, and chewed the tissue paper. Finally, Jack opened the bathroom door, scolded Eleazar, and again closed the door, leaving the light on. Not another peep was heard from the little guy for the rest of the night.

In the meantime, the manager's wife came on duty at midnight. As she scanned the register, her eyes read, "Llama in Room 7." She had never seen a llama, nor did she know what one was. She did know, however, that it was some kind of animal. The next morning, when the occupants of Room 7 exited, there she was. She had been chain smoking, nervously waiting to see what this llama would look like.

Jack and Dee had been home about a week when they received a postcard from the motel manager and his wife. "Dear Jack, Dee, and Eleazar," they wrote. "We certainly enjoyed your visit. Come and see us again soon!"

Tofooey

One afternoon in early December we received a telephone call from a building contractor friend. He wanted to know if we would consider allowing him to use our home for a Christmas dinner party for his crew. He would arrange to have it catered, he explained, and wanted it to be something extra special. He felt our place would be homey and informal. Since we had made no plans for that evening we told him we would be happy to host the party. He assured us that everything would be taken care of. All we needed to do was to supply the facility and enjoy the evening.

On the day of the party, I arrived home early. Barbara had left instructions that specific things should be readied because she couldn't leave her office until rather late.

I followed through, and managed to have things looking quite nice by 6 P.M. The guests were due to arrive at 6:30. The tables and chairs were set up, the floors had all had been vacuumed, and the china and silverware were in their proper location. We were all set!

I was hopeful that Barbara would arrive momentarily. I always feel more comfortable when the lady of the house is present for some gala affair such as this. Richard, our builder friend, had promised that the young chef, François, would arrive early to prepare the dinner. He would also have the punch and hors d'oeuvres.

Six thirty came and I was still by myself. Finally, at 6:45, Richard appeared.

"Isn't François here yet?" Richard asked. I shook my head.

"He'll be here any time," he promised.

Finally Barbara appeared. As she was frantically changing clothes, the first guests began to arrive. I made my way to the refrigerator and found some 7Up and pineapple juice. Placing the mixture in the punch bowl and finding some Valentine's Day paper napkins, I readied the serving area and began to serve the drinks. About that time, up the back steps came François, a look of frenzy on his face, his arms loaded with groceries. He had gotten stuck in the snow on his way to the party and had to get a tow truck to free him. Simultaneously, Barbara appeared and began to organize the confusion. In rather short order the kitchen was a beehive of activity, the guests were visiting and enjoying themselves, and the pleasant aroma of François' creations were fill-ing the air. I was beginning to feel quite relaxed and had begun to visit with our guests. At that moment, I felt a touch on my shoulder. It was Barbara.

"You have to run in to the store," she whispered. "François needs some Tofu."

I had never heard of the stuff. For a moment I couldn't figure out what she was talking about.

"He needs some what?" I said. "What in the world is tofu?"

"François will tell you about it," said Barbara. "Ask him, but hurry!"

The young chef quickly informed me that I would find it in the produce section at the store. "Please hurry," he said.

The night was dark. It had been snowing but had momentarily stopped. When I got to my car, I quickly observed that it was blocked by several other automobiles. There was no way I could get it out. However, François' car was free. I decided to use it. In the meantime, Richard had come to my assistance and was moving vehicles so I could get out.

François' car was an early model Buick that had seen better days. There was no dome light. The ignition wires had to be crossed in order to start the engine. As I fumbled to right myself in the driver's seat, I suddenly realized that I had sat in something. I quickly jumped out of the car. When I looked down, the entire back of my pants and upper left pants leg were covered with a dark, gooey, substance. I hesitatingly touched the stuff and slowly brought my hand to my nose to determine what it was.

"What in the world is that?" quizzed Richard, a perplexed look on his face.

"I. . . I. . . I'm not sure, but I think it's some kind of dessert," I stammered. "You'd better go get the tofu, Dick. I can't go anyplace."

In my attempt to use François' car, I had sat directly in the chocolate mousse that he had prepared for dessert. He hadn't told me that it was in his front seat. Of course, he hadn't known I was going to use his car; neither had I!

I silently sneaked up the stairs to the hallway and, standing with my back to the door, sheepishly asked one of the guests to tell Barbara I needed her. Then I slowly backed down the hallway to our bedroom. Barbara found me. She was horrified when I explained what had happened.

"What shall we tell François?" she groaned. "Oh, I can't believe this!"

She returned to the kitchen while I changed my pants. When she asked him what he was planning for dessert, he broke into a broad grin and proudly shook his head. "Oh," he said, "it's one of my specialities. I took special pains to make it for Richard's party. It is going to be delicious!"

It was then that Barbara asked him to show her where it was. As they approached the Buick, Barbara summoned the courage to explain what had happened. Almost hysterically, he opened the car door. As he extracted the remains of the mousse he began to smile slightly.

"This isn't too bad," he sighed. "We can salvage it."

He quickly laid both cake trays on the snow and began to reshape the contents. When he had finished, he washed his hands in the snow and carried the trays to the kitchen.

The dinner party was a tremendous success. The guests expressed profuse appreciation to Richard and complimented François, especially for the delicious dessert. To this day, they have no idea how François performed a miracle in the snow!

Alias Dr. Doolittle

When one buys a ranch he becomes popular with neighbors who want to get rid of animals.

Michael was a young man who owned a business in town. One day he asked me if I would like a couple of pygmy goats. Before committing ourselves, we went to see what they looked like. They were cute little rascals, and were brothers. About five months old, their horns had just started to form. Both had goatees. We chuckled—they resembled little old men. Barbara liked the idea of adding them to our growing menagerie.

"They'll keep the pasture trimmed," she beamed, "and they're so darling!"

I agreed. Michael seemed pleased to know that they would have a good home, so I brought them to Bigfoot. They adapted quickly to their new surroundings. Neither Jasper nor the llamas paid much attention to them. They seemed content to roam the pastures, freelancing to their hearts' content. Occasionally, they slipped through the fence, but in general, they remained inside their corral.

In a matter of weeks their horns began to grow. I hadn't realized they would eventually become miniature replicas of mountain goats. They were always butting each other, but they confined their antics among themselves.

That spring, as I was irrigating the front pasture, one of the sprinklers broke. I was leaning over endeavoring to fix it when it happened. I suddenly found myself flat on my face in the pasture mud. As I picked myself up, the inevitable became quite clear. Bent over as I was, I presented an irresistible target for one of the goats. When the opportunity came, he really "lowered the boom." Sheepishly, I looked around to see if anyone had been watching. I was relieved to see no one. The sight of a two-hundred-pound man being abruptly upended by a pygmy goat could easily have been something that I had to live with for the rest of my life.

My theory about neighbors wanting to relinquish their animals to us continued to gain credibility.

I was driving into town one day and happened to stop by to say see how my neighbor, Joe Lombardi, was doing. He had broken his leg a few days before when one of his steers jammed him in his corral.

"Say, Phil, how would you like some geese at your place?" he queried. "I can get you some!"

"I just might be interested, Joe," I responded.

The next day I visited Joe's friend, the owner of the geese. Joe asked me to drive out to his place.

"So you're the dude who wants some geese, eh?" he drawled as I drove up. "I've got four you can have— three drakes and a gander. But ya' can't have 'em now. I don't let my birds go when they're layin'. I'll call ya' in a couple weeks when they're ready."

Sure enough. In just two weeks he telephoned. "Ward," he began, "I've got some bad news for you. Your four geese have turned into ten! Bring some gunny sacks and come and get 'em."

When I arrived home with the four adults and six goslings, I quickly introduced them to their new home, a pen I had hastily constructed for temporary housing. I thought it would be a good idea to contain them in a restricted area for a short time until they became familiar with the surroundings.

In the meantime, other neighbors had presented us with a peacock and a peahen. They were gorgeous birds, fully matured and possessed vivid colors. They roamed free around the ranch.

The geese had been residents about a week when one day I noticed the peacock scrutinizing them from outside their pen. I surmised that he had not seen geese before. It was obvious he was perplexed. Spontaneously, he flew to one of the posts anchoring the pen. Then, without warning, he swooped down into the flock. They immediately rejected him, pecking at him furiously and, in general, expressing a considerable lack of hospitality. He helicoptered out as fast as he had entered, and flew a few yards where he landed next to his mate. I imagined him saying to her, "You'll never believe what happened to me!" And then, both approached the goose pen fence to view the occupants. I laughed to myself when I realized that they resembled humans viewing animals in a zoo.

When the geese had been penned for two weeks, it was time for them to explore the ranch. I opened the gate, and stood back to observe. Just as though they knew where they were headed, they began a single-file march down the pasture fence line. There were about fifty cattle feeding in our neighbor's field. As the geese continued, the cows suddenly stopped eating, meandered to the fence, and all stood staring, as though in disbelief, at the antics of the geese. The entire scene was hilarious. All that was missing was the discordant braying of Jasper!

A Trip to Revenuer Country

Once an individual leaves a profession he enjoyed for many years, there is the possibility that it can create a void in his life for some time. Both Barbara and I had been elementary educators for thirty years and felt we still had something to contribute to our community's youth. It was for this reason that soon after our move to Mt. Shasta we created Wards' Consulting Services.

I had the fortunate experience to contract with the County Superintendent of Schools to perform limited services to the schools of the county. My responsibilities included working in specific areas with all of the county schools.

The schools covered a wide geographical area. About one-third of them were one or two teacher schools, and located in extremely rural, isolated areas. One such school for which I was responsible was located about two hours' driving time from the County Schools Office. Located on one of the most scenic mountain rivers in that part of the state, the small community consisted of a post office, a grocery store, a saloon, and a small, one-room building which doubled as the community center and a school room for upper grade children. Each time I journeyed there, I was reminded of the movie, "Deliverance," filmed in the backwoods country of Kentucky. . . remote, cradled in a heavily forested mountain canyon, and approachable only by a one-lane dirt road or helicopter.

I had visited the school only twice when, in the late spring, I received a telephone call from the principal. "Phil," he began, "graduation is approaching. The kids have taken a vote and they would like to have you as their graduation speaker. Will you do it?"

I was taken somewhat off guard at his request, but rebounded enough to respond positively.

"How many graduates will you have?" I asked.

"Three," was the response.

"And how long would you like me to speak?"

"Anywhere from three to five minutes," he said.

When I hung up the phone, I found myself reflecting on my past graduation experiences. The last graduation I had attended was my last year at the junior high school where I had been principal. It had been a school of one thousand. There were over 500 in that last graduating class. I had not only addressed the graduates then, but had organized the entire affair, including several rehearsals and other preparations. There must have been an audience of at least 1500 parents, relatives and friends in attendance on that afternoon in June. This experience, indeed, would be a new and unusual one! On the special day, I arrived home from the office early to dress for the occasion. I had invited Barbara to go with me as she had never been to that part of the county. We donned dress apparel and headed west for the gala event. I made good time driving and we arrived in the little community about half an hour before the graduation ceremony was to begin. I noticed a sign in the saloon window advertising cheeseburgers. I asked Barbara if that sounded good to her and she said it did. As we were about to enter the tavern, I noticed three or four pickups parked in front.

Immediately I was reminded of the scenes from the "Gunsmoke" series that was on television years ago. This setting could easily have doubled for the "Long Branch Saloon."

"Now Honey," I said, "don't be surprised at anything when we walk through that door."

As we entered, three guys were shooting pool. Four others were sitting at the bar having drinks. All activity stopped and every head in the place turned to us when we opened the door. One of the pool players walked up, cue stick in hand, looked at both of us, and then, with a half-grin said, "Are you on the right road?"

"I hope so," I answered, as we made our way to the counter to order the cheeseburgers. While we ate I was engaged in conversation by a fellow sitting next to me.

He wanted to know why we were there. I casually mentioned that I did consulting for the county schools and that I was going to speak at the graduation ceremony. When he found out that I had something to do with the school, he began to severely criticize the teachers and the way the school was supervised. I listened, casually nodding my head periodically to let him know I was not ignoring him completely. As we finished our sandwiches and turned to leave, I said to my talkative neighbor, "You certainly seem to know a lot more about this school than I do. Maybe you'd like to give this graduation speech!"

"Not on your life," he blurted, "I wouldn't touch it with a ten foot pole!"

It was time for the ceremony to begin as we entered the community center. There were stacks of wood on the porch of the building. Wood was the main source of heat in that community. The building consisted of one room. As we entered we had to walk around two stacked fifty-gallon oil drums. They were welded together to form a wood stove. Benches were available for audience members. Two women were readying the refreshment area. Barbara and I sat down on one of the benches, feeling somewhat like revenuers in a strange and far-away land. Bare-bottomed babies and toddlers, apparently younger siblings of the graduates, were running around the room and over and between the benches. Family and friends were beginning to arrive.

When the principal saw us he quickly came forward and whispered in my ear. "Phil, we are having trouble with our generator and it will be a while before we are able to start the program."

"Please don't worry about us," I whispered back. "We have plenty of time."

In a short time the room was filled and we heard the generator start. The program was about to begin.

Three chairs had been placed in front of the room for the graduates. They were standing, dressed to the hilt, at the rear of the room. In preparation for the ceremony, a large box had been placed on the floor to serve as a podium. A long branch, angled over the top of the box, held a microphone.

The ceremony began. The primary grade teacher explained that some of the children had written poems about the graduates. He called on the first little boy to read his poem. The little fellow, rather hesitatingly, made his way to the microphone. Unfortunately, no one had thought about checking the height of the microphone compared to the size of the individual speaking. When the youngster began to speak, all anyone could see was his hair line. There were some chuckles. When the child heard people laughing, he ran from behind the box to the rear of the room. His mother immediately began to yell at him. "You get back up there," she screamed. The embarrassed boy became more even elusive.

"No, no," he yelled back. "I'm not going back up there!"

The scene was both hilarious and embarrassing. I wondered how something like this could happen, and my heart went out to that little guy. The teacher finally realized what was happening, and quickly ushered another child to the podium, making certain to place a block of wood from a nearby stack for this child to stand on.

The poems were delightful and in a short time the opening incident had been forgotten.

When the poems concluded, the principal introduced me. The graduates were still standing at the rear of the room.

"Since my remarks are going to be addressed to you," I said to the graduates, "I wonder if the three of you will please come to the front and be seated?"

Somewhat timidly they complied. When they were seated, I began. I told them how proud we all were and what a pleasure it was to see the looks of pride on their parents' faces. I also spoke about their accomplishments of the last eight years and the challenges they would be facing in the next four. My four minutes of allotted time went quickly, and I made sure that I ended promptly.

The principal then called on the graduates to speak. The first young man rose, introduced himself and briefly explained his plans for the future. "When I graduate from high school," he said with pride, "I'm going to be a logging truck driver." He then sat down.

The second graduate was a young lady. She wore a neat, colorful dress. A permanent hairstyle enhanced her image. She told where she was going to high school, proudly shared her dream of wanting to go on to college, and thanked everyone for helping her get this far in her education.

The last graduate was a young man who reminded me of the character "Alfalfa" in the "Our Gang" movies of the 1930's. His hair was combed flat with what appeared to be a layer of vaseline. His tie was showing over the collar of his coat. His smile, and his inward glow, however, completely fascinated me. When he spoke, you could have heard a pin drop. "First," he said, "I want to thank my parents for all they have done to get me this far. I really feel lucky that they want me to continue my education. I just hope that some day I will be able to repay them for their love and support." He ended his speech by thanking his teachers for their time and efforts in helping him reach this milestone.

I was flabbergasted! During my career in education I had heard numerous graduation speeches, but none had touched me the way this one had. I looked at Barbara. Tears were in her eyes. I quickly realized that she, too, was touched.

The principal said a few words about the graduates and then called on the School Board members to present the diplomas. Each member handed a diploma to the graduates.

"That ends the ceremony," announced the principal. "We hope you all will stay and share in refreshments with the graduates."

Barbara and I lingered for a short time, personally congratulating the graduates and their parents. We then left for the two-hour drive home.

We remember our trip vividly and often reflect on that experience. We both feel enriched as a result of being asked to share in what I consider the most memorable graduation experience of my life.

"OOM-PAH-PAH"

I had driven into town one afternoon in June to do some shopping. About noon I stopped in to visit my folks. They invited me to have a sandwich. As we were talking the subject turned to the Fourth of July celebration. It is always a popular and well-attended holiday in Mt. Shasta.

"You know," said Mom, "it's just a shame they don't have a band for the big parade. We haven't had a band for four years now."

"You're kidding," I responded. "What's a parade without a band?"

I had played in the high school and community bands in my youth and had thoroughly enjoyed it. I couldn't believe that there was no band.

"Well, we've got to do something about that," I said.

And while I was sitting at the table, I began jotting down the names of those high school classmates who played in the band and still lived in the area. I could remember eight. Dad knew of two or three community members who had played in the town band at one time or another. I thanked the folks for lunch and said goodbye. "I'll keep you posted," I yelled, and drove away.

When I told Barbara about my idea, she was encouraging. "You can count on me, too," she promised. "I'll have to get out my flute and see if I can still blow it." The last time she had played was in college. She hadn't touched it since then. I had an occasional opportunity to play my trombone while in Saratoga. I would periodically "sit-in" with the Junior High band.

The next evening I started to telephone those former band members whom I remembered. The reaction to my invitation was mixed. The first person I called asked me to repeat myself. "You've got to be kidding, Phil," he answered. "How can a guy play the trumpet with false teeth?"

The second fellow told me that he hadn't blown his tuba for forty years and that he had donated it to the school years ago.

I did, however, elicit some interest from four of my former classmates. They reluctantly agreed to think about the idea and asked me to keep them posted.

I contacted the local radio station and was interviewed. "The idea," I stressed, "is to get enough band members together to play in the parade. Our community deserves it and after all, folks, every parade has to have a band. Come and join us. We'll have a great time!"

That announcement, coupled with two or three articles in the local paper, brought significant results. I was able to talk a local composer into directing the band. We borrowed the local high school's band music and secured a semi truck and trailer from a community-minded trucker. Thirty-five participants showed up for our first rehearsal. By this time, however, it was close to the big day. We had just two rehearsals before the parade. Each member bought his own straw cowboy hat and red bandana. After the second rehearsal, we were ready!

Early on the morning of the 4th, several band members helped decorate the trailer. Banners lined each side with the words, "Mt. Shasta Community Band." They were outlined with red, white, and blue crepe-paper streamers. As we boarded the float, the cowboy hats and red bandanas made a colorful sight.

The band float was placed in the middle of the parade lineup.

It had been a beautiful morning, but close to the start of the parade, the clouds looked threatening. Then, as the parade began, the band let go with John Phillip Sousa's, "The Thunderer." Immediately, it began to rain. We couldn't believe it!

Fortunately, the rain was short-lived, and by the time we had tooted just two short blocks, the sun began to shine.

Mt. Shasta City is a community of about three thousand. However, this parade annually draws a crowd of twice that many spectators. As the band came into view, and the multitude crowding the curbs, lawns, and porches of the downtown area saw and heard the band, the reaction was glorious to behold. Men whistled, women clapped, and children ran and danced, touching the float at every opportunity. The reception was overwhelming. I sensed that each band member was having the same reaction as I was. Any showman will tell you that the performer is only as good as his audience—because of the reception that day, the Air Force Band of the Golden Gate couldn't have played any better at that instant.

There was so much enthusiasm by band members that we decided to continue the band. I started receiving calls from nearby communities to play for their festivities. One town offered one hundred dollars if we would march in their parade in uniform. We called a meeting of all members to discuss that possibility. "We already have our uniforms," I explained to the group. "How do you feel about marching?"

"Heck," replied one of the senior members, "I don't think my pacemaker can take it!"

By the end of summer, we had become a cohesive and well-rehearsed group. We knew we weren't "big time," but we also recognized that the resulting sound had considerable appeal. What we needed now was a permanent director, a practice facility, and a music library. The nearby community college was contacted, and after several meetings, the band was incorporated into the evening adult education program . As a result, the county now has a musical group representing the entire area to enhance the enjoyment for all.

A Chewed Blue Ribbon

One summer afternoon we received a telephone call from a lady in a nearby town. She explained that the elementary school children were having a pet parade the following day and asked if we would be willing to enter our llamas. "Many of the children have never seen a llama," she said, "and the committee heard about yours. Could you possibly bring them?"

We were pleased to be invited and accepted her invitation. Early the following day Barbara and I prepared "the boys" for their debut. First we tethered them, then combed and brushed them thoroughly. From their harnesses we hung colorful tassels. Bright bandanas were placed around their necks. We found two old straw hats and cut holes for their upright ears. When we had finished, they actually seemed quite proud of themselves. Off we went to the parade.

Now the hometown parades in this part of California are quite special. Usually, it's a time for the local fire department and county road department to show off their rolling-stock. Often, car dealers are represented, as well as the local drum and bugle corps. Children's baton classes add to the fun, too.

But this parade wasn't one of those. It was strictly a "pet" parade. It appeared that every child in town was there with their pet.

As I unloaded Eleazar and Bobbin, a little girl carrying a glass jar approached me. "What are those animals?" she asked.

"They are llamas," I replied. "And what do you have?" I countered.

"Oh, this is my pet butterfly," she said smiling. "I am going to be in the parade, too."

We took our position in the lineup. Barbara was leading Eleazar. I had Bobbin. As we walked down main street, our animals drew much attention. Both appeared to be enjoying their day in the sun. We were at the end of the second block when we passed a little girl in a wheelchair. Waving a bright colored flag, and smiling widely behind two missing front teeth, it was obvious that she was enjoying herself. Suddenly, immediately in front of the little girl, Barbara was jerked to a complete stop by Eleazar. Either the razzle-dazzle flag or the movement of the wheelchair must have momentarily caught his attention. In llama-like inquisitiveness, his ears stood straight up through the straw hat he was wearing. He looked directly at the little girl. Try as she might, Barbara pulled the rope to urge him forward. He wouldn't budge! The remainder of the parade behind us had stopped. Realizing that llamas like to stay together as they are being led, and thinking that it would solve the problem, I maneuvered Bobbin into position next to Eleazar. That idea failed. Barbara was becoming more embarrassed by the second; so was I. Finally, the little girl moved forwards and held her hand out to Eleazar, and moved closer to him. It suddenly became obvious that the animal was responsive to her. Not knowing what else to do, I quickly asked her father, who was standing next to her, if he would push her in front of Eleazar for the remainder of the parade. He nodded approval. Barbara handed the lead rope to her and for the rest of the parade Eleazar, without incident, followed the girl and her father.

At the end of the parade, all entries were awarded prizes. Eleazar received a blue ribbon for being the tallest animal in the parade. We hung it on his harness.

The llamas garnered much attention as we walked back up main street. One of my friends who had watched the passing parade stopped us. He was intrigued by the llamas and invited Barbara and Eleazar into his little art gallery. Barbara was hesitant to enter with Eleazar but Bill insisted. They quickly toured the small, one-room building. Eleazar gave his approval to most of the paintings, turned up his nose at others, and started to chew one vaguely resembling a goat. Barbara thought maybe it was his long-lost cousin. To this day we aren't sure whether my friend wanted to laugh or cry as a result of the visit.

When we arrived back at our Bigfoot Ranch and unloaded the celebrities, we noticed that Eleazar had chewed his blue ribbon. "Maybe he's miffed because he didn't win 'best of show'," said Barbara when she saw what happened.

We presently have pictures of both llamas hanging in our family room. The blue ribbon hangs from one corner of Eleazar's picture. When anyone asks about it, we simply smile and say, "It just isn't everyone who has a chewed blue ribbon!"

My Daddy Isn't Coming Home

My years in education have been glorious. I couldn't have chosen a profession I would have enjoyed more. One often hears that the pay isn't what it should be for teachers. That's not true. Why? Because it depends on how "pay" is defined. In reference to salary, it has always been difficult for me to understand why a higher priority hasn't been placed on the importance of teachers. After all, next to a child's parents, who spends the most time with our youth during their waking moments? And who can be more influential? When you think about the fact that the future of our country will be in the hands of our present school-age children in a few short years, what could possibly be more important than placing teachers in a top priority income bracket.

But if one considers the "payoff" for individual teachers, and those "treasures" that personally come to those who love children and really care about them, then they are blessed beyond measure!

During my years in Saratoga as the principal of an elementary school, I annually had the privilege of playing Santa Claus for all of the children in the district. The primary teachers would buy candy canes which were placed in the school office. Each school secretary would then place them in a pillowcase. When Santa arrived, he would take his bag and proceed to each classroom. It was always a gala occasion and the look of a small child receiving a candy cane and looking up into the eyes of Santa Claus is something that I shall cherish forever.

On one such occasion, Santa had entered the classroom and, after dancing a quick little round with the teacher and singing "Jingle Bells" (as only Santa can do), he suddenly felt a tug on his Santa-coat. Looking down, Santa saw a little first grade boy looking up at him. "Ho, ho, ho," laughed Santa, "hello, there, little fellow. And what can Santa do for you?"

Looking all the way up to Santa's eyes and smiling, the little guy replied, "Hello, Mr. Ward!"

"Oh," said Santa, "I'm not Mr. Ward. I'm Santa Claus."

"Oh, no, you're not," was the reply. "I'd know your shoes anywhere!"

One day I dropped in to visit one of my kindergarten classes. I loved these "little people" for many reasons. I found them fascinating. They are direct and honest. They are miniature adults, only much less inhibited and more natural. The children were engrossed in numerous activities in small groups. One little girl saw me immediately and enthusiastically ran to me. She grasped my hand and led me to a kindergarten-sized chair. She motioned for me to sit down. I wondered what was about to come. Maybe a new baby had arrived that she wanted to tell me about. Or perhaps the family was planning a trip. I even thought she might want to share that Grandma and Granddad had arrived for a visit. Instead, she sat me down, placed her darling freckled-face about three inches from mine, grabbed a loose front tooth with her little fingers, and blurted with pride, "Look, I've got a loose tooth!"

There are a multitude of other "warm fuzzies" I have experienced during my tenure in education. I cherish both the memories and thank the Lord for placing me in the profession He did.

The one most vivid in my memory happened when I was asked to assume the superintendency of a little school not far from Mt. Shasta. I was delighted to have the opportunity to return to a school in this capacity. It did not take long before I realized just how much I missed the direct association with school children.

I had been at the school about three weeks when one Friday morning an intercom call was received in the office. The fourth grade teacher asked that the principal come to her classroom as soon as possible. I sensed urgency in her voice so I proceeded, post haste. The teacher took me to one side and quickly whispered, "Phil, Jake just ran out of the classroom. I don't know where he went. He hasn't had a good day. His father was taken to jail this morning."

"I'm glad you called me," I responded. "I'll take care of it."

Being unsuccessful in finding Jake anywhere in the school building, I went outside. I soon found him sitting on a curb a the edge of the school grounds, chin in hand, and staring straight ahead. Sitting down beside him I gingerly placed my arm on his shoulder and asked, "Would you like to talk, Jake?" A shake of his head told me what I needed to know. He was too upset to talk. So I, too, sat quietly with him. I wanted to seek him out, but was at a loss to know exactly what to say. Finally, I thought of something. "You know, I didn't have any breakfast this morning, and I'm hungry. I think I could go for an ice cream cone. Would you like to join me, Jake?" He nodded in quick approval.

We got into my car and headed for town. The little community was small and had limited shopping facilities. I suddenly realized that I didn't know where to get an ice cream cone. "I'm not sure where we can get a cone," I murmured.

"You can get one right here," he blurted, just as we were passing a little neighborhood grocery store. I parked, purchased two cones, and together we sat in my car licking ice cream. Soon Jake began to open up.

"My Daddy was taken to jail this morning and he won't be home tonight," he volunteered.

"Your teacher mentioned something to me about that, Jake. What happened?"

"He was bringing my brother and me to school this morning when the Sheriff pulled us over and arrested my Dad. I don't know why. But we don't have any money to get him out of jail, so I know he won't be home tonight." He began to sob.

"I doubt that things are that bad, Son," I said quietly, placing my hand on his head. "I'll tell you what. When we get back to school, I'll check with the Sheriff's office to see how your Dad is doing. Would you like that?" A quick nod of his head accompanied by a child's grateful smile told me that he felt relieved.

When we returned to school I sought out the deputy who was in charge of the drug education program for the county. He was a fine man and had developed an excellent rapport with the children. During the short time we had worked together, a warm friendship had developed between us. I asked Dennis if he would check on Jake's Dad so we could know what was happening.

"Certainly," he responded. "I'll call the office now and find out what's going on."

In a few minutes he came into my office. "There's no major problem, Dr. Ward," he said. "Jake's Dad was picked up this morning because of an overdue traffic violation. His wife just picked him up and he's on his way home now. I thanked Dennis, and made my way to Jake's classroom at the next recess. As he exited the room I pulled him to one side and whispered privately to him. "Jake," I said, "you don't have to worry. Daddy will be home tonight. Your Mom picked him up just a little while ago."

The resulting smile would have melted an iceberg.

"Gosh, thanks, Dr. Ward," he beamed, and skipped out to recess.

The following Monday I was making some weekly announcements to each class throughout the school. When I entered Jake's classroom and was speaking to the class, my eyes met Jake's. He smiled at me, and, of course, I smiled back. He was wearing a white shirt and tie, a sportcoat, polished shoes, and sported a brand new haircut. I was impressed! At the next recess I met him in the corridor. "Golly, Jake, you look like a million dollars today. How come?"

His response floored me. "That's because I want to be like you," was his reply.

I spent the rest of the day in a state of shock. In all my years in education, I had never had anything hit me as directly as Jake's statement. I consider it one of the major "payoffs" of my career.

A Surprise at Midnight

As our Bed and Breakfast business began to grow, we decided to convert our old barn into a guest cottage. It was a well-constructed building but had never been finished. We knew what we wanted to do and proceeded to hire a local contractor to work with us. Being new to the county, I was uninformed about building codes and protocol. A number of friends advised that to simply convert an existing barn into a living unit did not require a county building permit. "Besides," advised one, "the more questions you ask, the more red tape you

have to contend with." Being anxious to complete the
project, we began the remodeling.

We had been working about three weeks when one
beautiful afternoon the county building inspector un-
expectedly graced us with his presence. "Well, well,"
he smiled. "What's going on here? It looks like you are
having a party and I wasn't invited!" I hastened to explain that I didn't think a simple conversion of a barn
to a cottage necessitated a permit, but he quickly
straightened me out on that point. He posted a "Stop
Work Order" on one wall of the building and as he left
informed me that we were not to proceed until I had
secured a building permit.

Four months later I understood what my friend had
meant when he referred to "red tape." During this time
we encountered numerous obstacles and discourage-
ment. I also became well acquainted with the Director
of the County Planning Department, the County Planning Commission, and the County Board of Supervi-
sors. However, recognizing that I had no one to blame
but myself, I charged it up to experience and considered it a lesson well learned. One hundred twenty-five
days later, we secured the permit.

Finally, the cottage was completely finished. The
transformation was remarkable. We now had a sepa-
rate living unit which would be ideal for an entire family or two or three couples. We furnished it tastefully
and on the day of the last furniture delivery, Barbara

and I opened a bottle of champagne to toast not only the new facility, but also our perseverance!

That night we were invited to dinner. We arrived home about 11:30 P.M. As we entered the house, Barbara looked at me with her dancing, beautiful brown eyes and suggested that we sleep in the cottage. "That would be neat," I happily responded. "You get our things together and I'll go out and start a fire." Taking a flashlight, I headed out the door. As I approached the cottage following the rays of the flashlight, I thought I noticed the front door ajar. On closer examination, I saw that I was right. What was this? The door had been forced open. I quickly turned on the lights. I couldn't believe what I saw. I blinked several times, thinking this must be some sort of dream. There wasn't a stitch of furniture to be seen. The sofa, day-bed, armoire, game table, and floor lamps were gone. I ran to the bedroom. The queen-sized bed, night stands, and over-stuffed chair were nowhere to be seen. The only evidence that there had been any furniture in the building was a small table lamp, one of a twin set we had purchased. As I was standing there, completely bewildered, Barbara suddenly appeared. For a brief moment, she did not realize what had happened. Then it hit her. She dropped the things she was carrying, walked slowly toward me, then scanned the bedroom. "Wha—what's happened?" she blurted. Still unable to respond, I began to gather my senses. "We've been robbed," I gasped. "I can't believe it!" And for a few short seconds, both of us stood, staring at each other in silence and shock. I finally gathered my senses enough to think about calling the sheriff, and in a few minutes he arrived. We explained the situation. He asked for a description of the furniture. We methodically enumerated what had been taken. "And I also want to tell you," I said, "that there was another little table lamp just like this one." He suddenly stopped writing, looked carefully at the lamp, and then, with a perplexed look, said, "Wait a minute. I just saw a lamp like that. On my way out here two fellows stopped me in a van and asked me for directions to an address on Deetz Road. As I was telling them how to get there I noticed that their van was full of furniture. The only thing I really saw was a table lamp. It looked just like that one!"

The three of us stared at each other for a split second in total disbelief. "Come with me," he blurted. "I think I know where your furniture is!"

The three of us jumped in his car and took off for Deetz Road, a rather isolated location about five miles from our ranch. "I'm sure I know where they were going," said the officer. "That house has been vacant for months."

In a few minutes we arrived at the house where he thought they might be. It was totally dark. The three of us walked up to the building. The sheriff tried the front door. It was locked. Shining his flashlight through the living room window, the three of us, with cupped hands to the glass, looked in. Then we raced to the bedroom window. We couldn't believe what we saw! The rays of the officer's flashlight revealed two complete rooms filled with our furniture. Every piece was arranged as though it had been there for months. The floor lamps were selectively placed. Even the queen bed was completely made with our quilted bedspread covering it. As we quickly window-scanned the other rooms, it was obvious that there was additional furniture besides ours.

"What do you suppose this is all about?" I queried.

"Well," he responded, "I can't say for sure, but it looks to me like someone is using this place to store stolen furniture. I'll get some additional help out here right now." In about twenty minutes, two other patrol cars arrived. Realizing that they had discovered foul play, they decided that we should first make positive identification of our stolen furniture. Since we had given the officer a detailed description of both the number of pieces taken and their description, all that remained was gaining entry to the building. The officers forced the front door open and turned on the lights. The interior was immaculate. The furniture, all new, had been arranged so that the interior gave the appearance of a tidy, beautifully cared for home.

After double-checking our furniture list and finding that everything was accounted for, the officers gave us permission to take our belongings back to the cottage. The deputy took us back to the ranch where were got our pickup and trailer. It was four o'clock in the morning when we completed moving all of our furniture back into the cottage.

We were contacted the following day by the sheriff's office and asked to present testimony to the District Attorney. We later were informed that the house containing the furniture had been rented under an alias and that the culprits had been apprehended. We were also told that they had been operating in neighboring states, apparently successfully, for the past two years.

Our cottage in the cedars has been in operation for five years and is increasing in popularity. We have never had another experience like that, however, and don't ever expect to!

A Memorable Trip to the "Tip"

Our eldest son, Jeff, married a lovely young lady from Sydney, Australia. Before the wedding we had the pleasure of having them live with us for six months. During that time Rose taught us an entirely new language. . . delightful Aussie sayings that most Americans haven't heard.

Not long after their arrival, I found it necessary to take a load of garbage to the local dump. I asked Jeff if he would like to ride there with me.

Overhearing our conversation, a perplexed Rose asked, "Where are you going?"

"I'm going to the dump, Rose," I replied.

"What's that?"

"It's a garbage dump, Rose."

"Oh," she responded, "at home we call that the 'Tip.'"

"The Tip," I quizzingly said, "where in the world do you get 'tip' from a garbage dump?"

"Well," was her reply, "when you get there you tip the garbage cans."

I looked at Jeff, shrugged, and said, "Let's go to the tip. It sounds a lot nicer than 'dump.'"

On the occasion of our 40th wedding anniversary, our sons honored us with a garden reception at our Bigfoot Ranch. It was a "no gift" affair; friends from the last 40 years were invited. Some guests, however, chose to bring gifts. One gift which was the highlight of the anniversary was a beautiful "friendship quilt" one of our favorite nieces had made. She had also incorporated pieces of precisely formed cloth for our friends to sign. She then planned to sew each one around the margin of the quilt. We were extremely touched by the gesture of love and time spent in making this exquisite work. Everyone marveled at the workmanship and the gorgeous selection of colors.

It was two days after the party before we had a chance to clean the house. The following Monday, both of us busied ourselves with the chores necessary to put the house back in order. I gathered up the garbage bags and other discarded residue from the party and headed for the tip. Upon returning, I continued helping Barbara with the vacuuming. I had almost finished when Barbara entered the room and asked, "Where are those boxes that were piled here on the hearth?"

"Honey," I replied, "I just took everything to the tip."

"You what?" she gasped. "The quilt was in one of those boxes!"

I was stunned. "I thought you put the quilt in the cedar chest in our bedroom. Are you sure you didn't?"

"No," stammered my wife. "It was right there on the hearth!"

"Holy smoke!" I gasped, starting toward my truck.

"Do you want me to go with you?" called Barbara.

"Honey," I answered, "you're still in your nightie. It would take too long for you to change," and off I sped.

About twenty-five minutes had elapsed since I had dumped the trash. Breaking all kinds of speed records, I raced back to the dump area like a mad man.

As I drew near the entrance, I saw in the distance a large garbage truck dumping its load in what looked like the same vicinity where I had discarded our trash. I couldn't believe it! Wildly, I drove past the grounds keeper shouting that I had to find something important. Sure enough, the truck had deposited its load exactly where I had thrown our waste. For forty-five minutes I proceeded to look through every kind of garbage imaginable. I waded in it well above my knees. I slipped in it. I crawled in it, and all the while, I didn't really know exactly what I was looking for. I had no idea what kind of a box the quilt was in or if it was even in a box. Finally, in desperation and near tears, my thoughts turned to the idea that maybe the quilt hadn't really been thrown away. . . maybe it was just in a different location back at the house. I returned home, and as I approached, Barbara ran to me with an anxious look and wanted to know, of course, if I had found it.

"No, I couldn't find it," I answered. "Are you sure it isn't somewhere around here?"

"No," she adamantly exclaimed, with tears in her eyes. "It absolutely is not here. Honey, we just have to find it!"

By this time she was dressed and again off we sped.

This time, we found that during the brief time I was gone, someone had dumped several rolls of old carpeting directly on the spot where I had been searching. While Barbara continued to search, two of the groundsmen assisted me in trying to move the rolls of carpet. We searched for about twenty minutes. Suddenly, Barbara called to me. I quickly looked in her direction. She was openly crying, but held a dilapidated and bent white box. Through her tears and babbling, I was able to decipher what she was saying. "Honey," she bawled, "I just asked God to please help us find the quilt. . . that we just had to find it, and when I opened my eyes I stepped right on this box!" In a split second I was standing next to her, staring in disbelief!

"You mean," I choked, "that you found the box? Is there anything in it?"

"Yes," was her tearful response. "Everything is here including all the name patches everyone signed. And the quilt is perfect!"

There we were, two grown, supposedly mature adults, wrapped in each other's arms, openly crying in the middle of the tip.

As we drove home neither of us could speak. The thought that God had responded to Barbara's prayer in the way he did was overwhelming.

Since that day at the tip, we have often wondered what anyone visiting the tip on that Monday morning must have thought.

'Round the Horn

Some might think that returning to one's hometown after an absence of thirty years would be "Dullsville." My hometown had changed somewhat, but as far as I was concerned, it was still the delightful little community I enjoyed in my youth. Returning to the little town at the foot of awe-inspiring Mt. Shasta brought back a multitude of joyous memories. I had truly found my little piece of heaven. I soon discovered that my home county had not changed much, either. It is one of the northernmost counties in California. Its primary industry has been lumbering. On the west, it is bounded by the Trinity Alps and the Marble Mountains. To the east, the Cascade Range zig-zags clear to Oregon. There are still some relatively "undiscovered" areas that California's vast populace has not invaded. I was soon to be reintroduced to one such location.

I contracted with the County Superintendent of Schools to assist his office in serving all the schools in the county which received specific funds from the state and federal government. Specifically, I was hired to assist schools in writing school plans to effectively use these "categorical" funds. This necessitated my becoming acquainted with the principals in each of the schools.

Soon after arriving at the County Office the first week of the school year, I was invited to tour the most remote schools in the county. My mentor was a gentlemen who was the Associate Superintendent and an experienced educator. We soon discovered that our careers over the years closely paralleled each other and we shared a great deal in common. Consequently, a positive rapport developed between us.

He issued the invitation. "Well, Phil," Clark smiled, "I must take you 'round the horn. You will find it most interesting."

At the time, I wasn't sure what he meant. I soon found out!

"Meet me here at the office at 7:30 tomorrow morning and I'll show you some beautiful country," he mused.

Bright and early the next morning we left the county office and headed west. The Klamath River runs from east to west, all the way to the ocean. We followed the river for the next two hours. It was a beautiful drive, and the highway meandered around and through and up and down, following the course of the river. It was the fall of the year and the colors were magnificent. Before we arrived at the sleepy little community of Happy Camp, the largest community on this state highway, we stopped at two small elementary schools where Clark introduced me to appropriate school personnel.

Happy Camp is primarily a lumber town situated directly on the Klamath River in a deep canyon surrounded by tall, heavily forested mountains. With a population of 2500, it is the last town of any size before reaching the coast and Highway One.

After leaving the elementary school there, we continued thirty-five miles before leaving the highway to head up the Salmon River. As we left the main road, Clark smiled and said, "Now where we're going will make the highway we just left look like the Los Angeles Freeway."

He wasn't kidding. The road rather abruptly changed from a two-lane paved surface to a one-lane, graveled path. We continued, and began to climb. I found myself looking down hundreds of feet into the Salmon River.

Clark quickly glanced in my direction and asked, "What do you think?" My reply never left my mouth, for as we turned a sharp corner, directly in front of us and pointing in our direction, were the remains of a logging truck. Standing beside the cab was the driver, a young man who looked to be in his early thirties. He was as white as a ghost. Clark immediately stopped and both of us approached the frightened man. Clark spoke first. "Are you all right? What in the world happened?"

He told us that this was his first trip on this road and that in negotiating one of the corners he had swung too wide and one of his rear wheels had overshot the roadbed. When that happened, the weight of the logs was too much for the rest of the trailer and they rolled off the rig, twisting it free from the cab. The logs had careened down the bank into the river. We walked to the edge of the road and looked over the embankment. Three hundred feet below lay the trailer, partially submerged in the river, wheels upright, the logs loose and clogging a portion of the river. It was easy to understand why the driver was tongue-tied. If the trailer had not wrenched loose from the cab, it would have destroyed both the cab and the driver.

While we stood there wondering what we could do to help, a second truck approached, laboring slowly around the sharp curve. This driver was an experienced logger and quickly assessed the situation. He assured us that help would arrive soon, so we continued on.

It was close to noon when we arrived at one of the occasional Forest Service campgrounds bordering the Salmon River.

"Well," mused Clark, "it's time for lunch."

We drove down an incline to a secluded picnic area. The river was not more than twenty feet away. Dogwood shrubs surrounded us and, although past their peak, they still retained their luminescent colors. Two mischievous gray squirrels were chasing and sassing each other as we readied the table. Clark opened the trunk of the car. He began to extract numerous tidbits. "This is a special occasion," he smiled. "We'll have a relaxing lunch and then head up river to the other schools."

I could not believe what this man had brought for lunch. First, he unfolded a small table cloth and spread it on the table made of rough-hewn fir timbers. Next, he placed a double candelabra, complete with candles, on the table cloth. When he started placing his assortment of food in front of me, my eyes must have been as big as silver dollars! He had brought salmon pate, kosher dill pickles, mushrooms, selected boxes of imported crackers, three kinds of cheese, and several scrumptious sandwiches which his wife had prepared especially for this trip. As we sat down to partake, Clark suddenly realized something was missing. Momentarily excusing himself, he returned to the trunk of the car and produced two crystal champagne glasses and a bottle of a bottle of chilled cider. At that moment, I felt like royalty.

For the next thirty-five minutes we immersed ourselves in delightful conversation and delicious food. As we sat there, thoroughly enjoying ourselves, and without a care in the world, my thoughts turned to what we must look like. Two grown men, miles from civilization, in the bowels of the Trinity National Forest, enjoying gourmet food in the middle of the wilderness. Absolutely hilarious!

By the time we had made our way to the last school on the river, it was mid-afternoon.

About eighteen miles further up river is located a school called Forks of the Salmon. It was a delightful little two-room school with approximately 40 students. We stopped there briefly to meet school personnel and then proceeded on up river. When we began our drive home, we were hot and thirsty. The sparkling cider was now only a memory.

As we slipped through the little community of Sawyer's Bar, I suggested that we get a cold drink at the local grocery. Clark welcomed the idea and parked in front of the store. As we were standing at the counter, a young lady was paying for groceries in front of us. She was dressed in a shirt and levi's. As she turned to leave, I noticed a large six-shooter strapped to her hip. It caught me by surprise. As unobtrusively as possible, I nudged Clark and motioned toward the gun. He was flabbergasted. As she drove away we asked the store owner about her.

"Oh, she's the local sheriff," he explained. "And believe me, she really knows how to use that gun."

It is a two-hour drive from Sawyer's Bar to Yreka. As we headed back to the office, I shared with Clark how much the day had meant to me. I had told him earlier that I had fought forest fires in that area of the county but an absence of thirty years had dimmed my memories of the beauty and remoteness of that portion of my home territory.

This trip reestablished my awareness of the glorious county in which I live. I indeed feel blessed to be back home in Bigfoot Country.

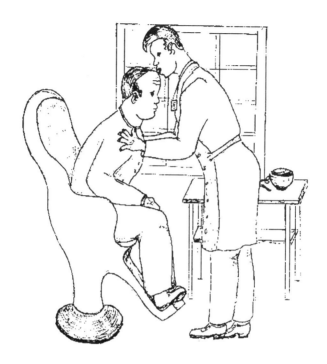

Oh! My achin' tooth!

Some people, unfortunately, never experience the blessing of having a real friend come into their lives... someone who can really be trusted. . . one who is your confidant and truly understands you. Well, I have! I never had a brother, but if I were given the opportunity to choose one, he would be Don Thompson.

Don was a successful, practicing dentist when I first met him. Our families became acquainted when we were in the same baby-sitting cooperative. Over the years our friendship grew and we found ourselves enjoying each other's company increasingly as our children shared school experiences. Our wives likewise became extremely close and our friendship developed into a relationship that both couples cherish.

Don's sensitivity and love as an individual made him highly revered and popular. He was our family dentist. Often when I would visit his office, we would share recent experiences related to a variety of things.

It was a rainy day a short time ago when one of the funniest things ever happened in my life. I developed a toothache and called Don's office for an appointment. They could take me immediately. When I arrived, his nurse guided me to the dentist's chair. Don soon entered and greeted me in his usual jovial manner. He usually had some joke to share which he seldom was able to finish telling before breaking into complete hysteria laughing at his own joke. Sometimes the stories were really funny. Most of the time, however, they left something to be desired. Often, at the height of the story, he would forget the punch line. I would laugh anyway. . . more because of his reaction to telling the story than the story itself.

"Buddy," he said excitedly, "you won't believe what happened to me on the way to the office this morning!" He was in dead earnest and shaking his head in apparent disbelief. It appeared that he had momentarily forgotten about my aching tooth. His attitude immediately caught my attention.

"What happened, Don?" I groaned, holding my jaw but sensing an urgency about his voice.

"Well, you know me well enough to know that I never pick up strangers. In fact, I've never given a hitchhiker a ride in all the years I've been driving. But this morning, it was raining cats and dogs and just as I passed the first intersection past my house, I saw this guy standing in the pouring rain thumbing a ride. He had a knapsack on his back, was bareheaded, and soaked. My heart immediately went out to him so I stopped and told him to hop in. I hadn't driven more than two blocks when he suddenly slid over toward me and put his hand on my knee."

"You've got to be kidding," I blurted, momentarily forgetting about my tooth, too.

"No, that's the honest to God's truth," replied Don.

By this time, Don had my complete attention. I had never seen him so serious.

"Well, for Pete's sake, what happened?"

He continued, "Well, never having had anything like this happen to me, I was flabbergasted. My instinct prevailed and I told the guy that he was getting out at the next corner."

"How come?" the guy snarled.

"Because that's as far as you go, " Don replied.

"As I stopped the car," said Don, "this character, obviously disgruntled, opened the door and started to exit. However, as he did he opened his knapsack, obviously searching frantically for something."

Don continued, sensing that he had my full attention. "At this point I thought sure I was a goner. I was
sure he was pulling a gun. He suddenly turned to me
with a can of some kind of spray, and sprayed my shirt
and coat and yelled, 'Ha, ha. . . in just a short time
you're going to be just like I am' and then slammed the
door."

"Holy cow, what a weird experience," I exclaimed.

"Yeah," answered Don. "I've been trying all day to
get this smell out of my clothes. It's a peculiar odor.
Here, smell my shirt."

As he said that he moved toward me so I could be
in a better position to smell. I leaned forward to sniff
his shirt and as I did, he kissed me on the forehead. He
immediately fell apart in complete hysteria, to say nothing of my reaction. Eventually, he did take care of my
aching tooth, but he had to cancel his appointments for
the remainder of the day.

The Unrecognized Treasure

My wife, Barbara, unfortunately suffers from a malady known as "Elementary School Teachers' Syndrome." A more common name for the affliction is "Pack Ratitus." It appears to be genetic in derivation, but is also fostered and encouraged in most teacher training institutions, and if one is not extremely careful, it can be contagious. I have determined that it is irreversible. Fortunately, I have managed to elude it. That is really a Godsend because if both of us had it, the house would have had to be annexed. Individuals with this disease have a tendency to collect items the average person could never imagine. Used milk cartons are one of their favorites. Another gem is used bottle caps. Old Christmas cards and discarded wallpaper book samples are also in demand. Extremely popular are used thread spools, toilet paper cores, and old light bulbs. Our garage walls are presently lined with

life-sized cardboard caricatures of "Joe Palooka,"
"Mandrake the Magician," and "Blondie and Dag-
wood." To illustrate the severity of the problem, four
years ago Barbara returned home from an area flea
market with a 1938 edition of a Speed Reading kit. To
this day it has not been used, and I truly believe that
she has even forgotten where it is stored. To be per-
fectly honest, most anything that doesn't move is subject to the magnetic fingers of these well-meaning
individuals.

One day when I was suffering from a memory lapse,
I foolishly asked Barbara if she would like to ride to
the local garage dump with me. She enthusiastically
accepted. To this day, I still don't know why I didn't
realize my mistake. When we arrived there, I got out of
the truck and started to unload the trash. Barbara slipped
out of the truck when I wasn't looking and began to
explore. Naturally, she was thrilled! Before I even realized where she was, she called to me.

"Oh, honey, look at this!" There was a tone to her
voice that I had heard many times and one which never
particularly thrilled me.

"Yes, dear, what is it?" I annoyedly replied.

"Come over here. It's a darling wrought iron bed.
And just look! It even has the rails that go with it. It's
just what we need for our little honeymoon cottage."

"Now look, sweetie, that's the last thing we need.
It's just a piece of junk!"

"Oh, no, it isn't either," she replied. "It's an absolute treasure! When we paint it, it'll be cute as can be."

Well, the stronger personality in the family prevailed and, of course, the bed went back to the ranch with us. I immediately stored it out of sight in our barn and for many months I hoped and prayed that it had been forgotten.

One December, about a year later, our church was going to have a rummage sale. To my surprise, Barbara suggested that we should take that old wrought iron bed to the church. "After all," she reasoned, "it is really an unusual size and we probably would never be able to use it."

I couldn't believe my ears, but I didn't wait for her to think about it a second time. I quickly backed the truck up to the barn and, with vim and vigor, loaded it ecstatically and delivered it to the church.

"Oh, joy," I said to myself, as I drove happily away from the church, "now some other lucky person will be able to have this 'jewel.'"

About three weeks after Christmas, I delivered considerable debris along with our well-used, dried-out Christmas tree to the dump. And since I was going into town afterwards, Barbara rode with me. As we approached the area where we were to unload our residue, I could not believe my eyes! I quickly nudged Barbara and both of us stared in disbelief. There, in precisely the same spot as we had found it months earlier, was the same wrought iron bed! Barbara still cannot understand why the local connoisseurs of rummage and garage sales overlooked that treasure. But I sure can!

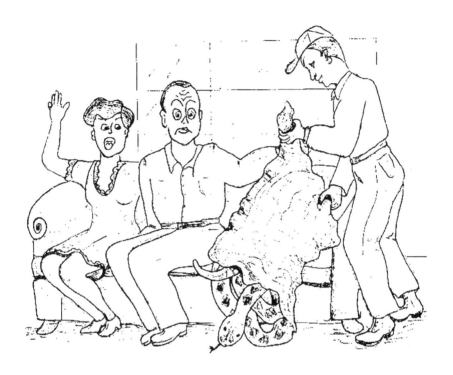

Toot, Toot, Tootsie, Good-bye!

Most people I know are not terribly fond of snakes. I fall into that category. I did, however, manage to hide my true feelings for reptiles when I was teaching because a teacher's attitude strongly influences his students. I vividly remember one of my sixth grade students inviting me to his home one day to see his pet; he said he wanted to surprise me. When I arrived at his home, he led me into the bathroom. There in the tub was a baby alligator. John was thrilled to show me his pride and joy. Fortunately, my limited acting ability surfaced and I was able to maintain my composure long enough to convince John that I was thrilled that he would share his pet with me. Needless to say, my visit to his home was rather short.

We had had our Bed and Breakfast for eight years when, one day, a close friend called us. He was a wonderful person and the type of individual who would do anything for his friends. He had helped us on numerous occasions in a variety of ways. He was being transferred to another part of the state and it would be about six weeks before he would be settled into his new home. He wanted to know if we would take care of his pet boa constrictor during that period of time. "I know this is asking a lot of you guys," Avery said, "but she is really no trouble at all. She's as gentle as can be, and after she eats she hibernates for about six weeks. I'm really in a bind. There is no pet store in the area and the animal hospital refuses to provide board and room for her. My only other alternative is to try to find a home for her and I don't have time to do that! Could you possibly help me out?"

"Oh, my Lord," gasped Barbara after the telephone call. "I can't believe that he'd ask us to do that! What in the world shall we tell him?"

Frantically, we tried to seek an alternative, both for Avery and for us, but we could think of nothing other than Avery's solution. The one positive note, we acknowledged, was the timing of his request. It was good because we had temporarily closed our Bed and Breakfast while we were remodeling our living room. After considerable discussion, we called him and told him that we thought we could manage as long as it wouldn't be longer than six weeks. He assured us that it might even be sooner and thanked us profusely. "I'll deliver her in the morning," beamed Avery.

Neither Barbara nor I slept well that night. Somehow, the thought of having a six-foot snake in our home was not conducive to rest and relaxation.

The next morning, Avery arrived with a large gunny sack containing "the Thing." When he rang the front doorbell and I opened the door, I froze! I had never seen so much bulk! "Hi," glowed Avery, and lifting the sack with both hands, stepped into the living room and plopped it on the carpet. He untied the sack and gently pulled and tugged the long greenish body slowly out of its temporary home. As he did, Barbara and I stood in absolute amazement at the size of the huge creature. I had never seen such a large snake.

"Phil and Barbara, meet Tootsie Roll. I wasn't able to readily find a cardboard box big enough for Tootsie Roll to sleep in," remarked Avery, "but I'm sure you can find an old refrigerator box in town at Robert's Furniture. They always have extra ones around." And then, almost as an afterthought, Avery smiled and mused, "Oh, I should also tell you that she doesn't eat much. I just fed her yesterday so she shouldn't have to eat again until I get back. She's very gentle, and kind of grows on you after awhile."

Lying there, fully elongated on our living room carpet, her camouflaged body resembled a fire hose filled with pulsating water. Avery explained that boas constrict when they are nervous or excited, and their bodies tend to increase in size. I gingerly touched the sinewy, tough, cartilaginous mass of muscle and immediately felt intimidated. Second thoughts about the wisdom of our offer flashed through my mind, but I realized that it was too late.

"I don't want you folks to worry about a thing," he said in a consoling voice. "I've had Tootsie Roll for two years and she's as tame as a kitten. Have fun!" Not knowing whether to laugh or cry, and endeavoring to hide our grief, we bid farewell to Avery.

"I'll tell you what, honey," I said weakly to Barbara, "I'll run down to Robert's and get a box."

"Oh, that's great," moaned Barbara. "You mean you're going to leave me alone?"

"Think of this as a thrilling new experience, dear," I smirked and headed for the furniture store.

That night we put Tootsie Roll in her box in one of our bedrooms. It filled the entire room! The next morning she was still there and apparently hadn't moved a muscle.

For four weeks, Tootsie Roll was a model guest. She slept constantly and our concerns about her began to subside.

Then one morning it happened! I was getting dressed when I heard Barbara shriek.

"Oh, no," she gasped, "I can't believe it!"

"You can't believe what?" I retorted, one leg in my pants and the other out.

"Tootsie Roll is gone," wailed Barbara, "I've searched the entire house!"

Together, we searched frantically for an hour. She was nowhere to be found. "Where can a six-foot snake possibly hide?" I kept saying. "She's got to be in the house someplace!"

"Could she have possibly gotten outside?" wailed Barbara.

"No," was my response. "Both of us have been very careful to keep the outside doors closed constantly. . . haven't we?"

We redoubled our efforts. Every day, for two weeks, we retraced our tracks. When we had searched everywhere without any luck, I called Avery. His reaction was low key and unconcerned. "I wouldn't worry about it, Phil," he said. "She will stay where it's warm and quiet." And then he added, "oh, incidentally, I forgot to tell you and Barbara. There is a possibility that she might be pregnant!"

I almost dropped the phone.

"Pregnant," I moaned. "You can't be serious. How many babies can a boa constrictor have?"

"Up to fifty," answered Avery.

I hung up and sank slowly in my chair. The thought of a pregnant snake, loose in our home, about to give birth to fifty babies was absolutely paralyzing!

Rededicated, we renewed our search. Ten days had passed since she had disappeared. Since our efforts had proved fruitless, we decided to continue our living room remodeling. Among other things, we had added two bay windows to the room. A window seat, unfinished at that point, had been built under one of the windows. Stereo speakers were to be installed under the seat.

One of the speaker compartments had a six-inch hole in the front which would eventually be covered with a grate to hide the speaker. As I knelt down to sand the lower portion of the window seat, I noticed a multicolored object in the inside corner of the cabinet. Upon closer examination, I realized that what I saw was a portion of Tootsie Roll's body. Retrieving a flashlight, I gingerly peeked into the hole. There, coiled in a tight circle, next to the warm wall which housed a heater on the other side, was Tootsie Roll, sound asleep. She had crawled out of her temporary bedroom home, across the hall and into our living room, and had deposited herself in a secluded and warm locale. The hole was barely six inches in diameter, and how she had gotten her immense body through that hole was more than I could fathom. There was no way I could get to her without removing one entire portion of the seat. I quickly looked for signs of babies and, seeing none, momentarily gave a loud sigh of relief.

Knowing very little about the habits of snakes, especially boa constrictors, I was at a loss to know how to remove her from her new-found home. Barbara frantically searched the encyclopedia for ideas. She found that when boa constrictors are hungry they eat live rodents. "Um," I thought. "It's been almost six weeks since she ate. Maybe we can lure her out with some live food."

A quick trip to a pet store in Yreka provided the necessary food. Upon returning I proceeded to place the rat in front of the hole, hoping that Tootsie Roll would be enticed to come out. As we watched, wondering what she would do, her head suddenly appeared in the opening and in a split second she grabbed and swallowed the rat! "My heavens," gasped Barbara, "look how big her throat is? She'll never be able to get back through that hole!"

She was absolutely right. Not only had Tootsie increased the diameter of her throat, but she was beginning to constrict again just as she had done when she made her initial introductory appearance in our living room. I finally determined that in order to free her I would have to take the stereo compartment apart. Working as gently as possible in order not to unduly disturb our pampered guest, I was able to finally gain access to her mammoth body.

Carefully and methodically, I proceeded to uncoil the mass of muscle, endeavoring to keep her as comfortable as possible. When I had finished, she lay stretched out on our living room carpet, apparently unperturbed by my antics. Gently, I prodded her with a broom handle and was able to guide her back to her box.

Suddenly, the humor of our predicament hit Barbara and, covering her mouth with her hand, blurted, "Honey, tell me how much fun we're having, will you? Nobody will ever believe this happened to us!"

I think the only other time in our married lives that we were this frustrated was the time when we were laying outdoor carpet on our deck and we started to lay it crooked, getting the carpet prematurely stuck and both ending up in the sticky mastic, botching the entire job!

The following week, Avery, in an answer to our prayers, arrived to pick up his pride and joy. He broke into a loud guffaw when we shared what had happened. Then, expressing his appreciation, he departed with our star boarder.

> Oh, somewhere in this promised land
> the sun is shining bright.
> The band is playing somewhere,
> and somewhere hearts are light.
> And somewhere men are laughing
> and somewhere children shout.
> But no more snakes at Bigfoot. . .
> No, sir, count us out!

The Fun of Owning a B&B

Shortly after we opened our Bed and Breakfast, a couple called to make reservations. Barbara took the call and explained that we would not be home when they arrived but the lights would be on and that they should come in and make themselves at home. She gave them what she thought were accurate directions to our home. Since they weren't arriving until after dark, Barbara explained that the lights would be on and we would be home shortly after dark.

When we arrived home later that evening our guests were comfortably seated in our living room and were enjoying themselves. Our guests were Chinese and this visit was their first to the United States. They were a delightful couple and we talked until almost midnight.

The next morning, as we were visiting during breakfast, they told us that they had something to share. Fortunately, these charming guests had a great sense of humor. They explained that the night before they inadvertently passed our home and drove down Hill Road until they came to what they thought was the Bigfoot Ranch. The lights were on in the house and the door was open. Taking their suitcases into the house, they placed them in the living room and made themselves comfortable. They had been there about half-an-hour when the gentleman happened to glance at the coffee table and see an envelope addressed to our neighbor. He realized that it was not the name he had seen on our brochure; he suddenly had the uneasy feeling that maybe they were in the wrong house. As quickly as possible, they picked up their suitcases and made a hasty exit. They retraced their tracks and fortunately soon found our residence.

Neither Barbara nor I have ever revealed that experience to our neighbor. However, we often wonder what might have been the consequences if our guests had gone to bed and our neighbor would have arrived home and found these strangers in his bed!

It was just a few weeks later when another rather unusual incident happened. We had just converted an old barn on our property into a delightful guest cottage and had not had a chance to advertise it. One day, shortly after its completion, we journeyed a few miles north to visit our son and daughter-in-law. Before leaving, we secured our property and the last thing I did was to close the gate at the entrance to our home. It was midnight when we returned. When I got out of the car to open the gate, I noticed that the cottage lights were on. Perplexed, I asked Barbara if she remembered leaving the lights on in the cottage when we had finished cleaning. She was sure she hadn't. We parked the car in the garage. It was dark when I closed the garage door. Suddenly a voice from out of the darkness startled me.

"Well, hello!" rasped the voice.

Bewildered, I answered with a feeble "Hello," and followed with, "who are you?"

"I'm John Everett," he replied, "and we're in your cottage."

"Oh, my gosh, did we book you and then forget that you were coming tonight?" I asked.

"No," he answered. "We just drove over from the coast and happened to hear about your cottage so we moved in."

I was astonished. I could not believe that anyone would have the nerve to enter a residence when it was obvious that it was closed and no one was home.

Barbara and I quickly made our way to the cottage. As we approached, a young lady met us at the door still drying her hair. It was obvious that they had moved in with all their gear, uninvited and without reservations.

My blood began to boil. Disgusted, but endeavoring to maintain my composure, I said to them, "You folks are assuming an awful lot. What would you do if we had this cottage already booked for tonight?"

"Oh, we didn't even think of that," replied John. "Is it reserved for tonight?"

"Fortunately for you it isn't," was my reply. "And this cottage rents for $90 per night."

"That's just fine," he chirped.

As Barbara and I made our way back to the main house, I grumbled something about how much gall some people had to do something like these kids had done.

"I'm going to have a real heart-to-heart with those two tomorrow at breakfast," I grudgingly said to Barbara. Then she smiled in her usual loving way and murmured something like, "Now don't raise your blood pressure, dear. Remember, you were young once and in love, too."

When the couple came to breakfast the next morning they were most apologetic. It was apparent that they realized they had taken too much for granted. Their attitude impressed me and we all decided that it was a growing experience for each of us.

We often reflect on these two rather peculiar experiences and realize that we are in a people-oriented business that always offers new and challenging experiences that keep life interesting.